The
PROPHET'S
STAR

Realm of the Prophets
Book III

E J Doble

Also by E J Doble:

THE BLOOD AND STEEL SAGA
The Crown of Omens
1: *The Fangs of War*
2: *The Horns of Grief*
The Knife of Sorrows

REALM OF THE PROPHETS
1: *The Crescent Moon*
2: *The Jade Sun*
3: *The Prophet's Star*

GRIMDARK FAIRYTALES
1: *Gold, Lock and Key*
2: *Pigs to Slaughter*

Copyright © E J Doble
All rights reserved
ISBN: 9781036927776

Cover design and illustration by:
Liam Fraser @lafgraphic

For Mum and Dad,

Thank you for fighting for who I am,
and reminding me of who I can strive to be.
I love you both so much.

Five years had passed, since the citizens of Arbash left their home on the outskirts of the Unknown. Five years had passed, since the people had gathered their lives and belongings, to traverse the distant sands and towering plateaus in search of somewhere else to live. In that time, the huge walls and wide stone streets of the city had become abstract memories: like the Prophets who had built it, the city had become part of a legend sung around campfires and whispered to children before they slept. Describing a city of lofty citadels and beautiful bronze-domed rooftops. Fields of clementine bushes, stretching down into a valley with a cove of painted stones at its base. To the elders, the memories were laced with nostalgia and melancholy; to the children, the tales gave them sweet dreams of market stalls and hummingbirds.

Travelling across the dunes of the Unknown, the memory of Arbash had followed them: both as a pleasant reminder of life before, but also as a fear of what would come next. Arbash had been their home. For the majority of its citizens, it had been the only one they had ever known. The life of nomads – seeking out wells and oases over the sprawling sands – had not been their way of life for generations.

It was a fear that had deep roots, borne of a life of comfort. They had been taught in their learning chambers when they were infants that the Unknown was as it was stated: a beyond, so unfathomably large that cartographers had never mapped it. To cross it was impossible – for what could one cross, if there was no end? To navigate it using the stars, was to seek a destination that did not exist. Their abandonment of the city – the place they had always called home – had been done on blind hope, illustrated to them by a young girl wrestling with her own understanding of life. Regardless, they had believed in her words, and with their God-Elect as vanguard they had trekked out into the beyond.

And by some miracle – as if by the Prophets' own hands – they had survived the journey. They found an oasis, in the heart of the Unknown.

And thus, New Arbash was born.

For many in the beginning, it had been a challenge to settle in a place so unlike anything they had experienced before. To scavenge for supplies, both at the water's edge and on the rolling dunes beyond. To place those first foundation stones, atop which would rise storehouses and workshops: the amenities that had once been taken for granted, which now grew from their own calloused hands. Like farmers, they had learned to tend the oasis, tilling soil for crops. Like healers, they had utilised the palm trees for ointments and bindings. Like hunters, they had set traps for prey out on the dunes, and bred the fish in the waters to keep their stocks secure. No matter the age or the status of each member, they had all strived towards that same goal: to survive, and give their little village the chance to grow into something better.

Hope had driven them into the desert, and community had held them together despite the odds. And after five years, New Arbash was a place that they could finally call home.

But it begged the question: a home for *who*, with what future out on the sands?

The citizens of Arbash, after so long out in the Unknown, no longer identified themselves in the same way: they were not of Arbash, and were no longer 'citizens' of any one place. The moniker of 'home' – once so gracefully applied to their former city – was now more of an idea, loosely attached to their new settlement and their place as those living in it. But it was *who* they actually were, and what that entailed, that now occupied space in their minds. They had, like tumbleweeds, travelled a great distance from one place to another, but in that transit they had also become something different, something *new*. They were not the same people, in belief or profession, who had once strolled the wide promenades of Arbash. They were not the same people who had tended the olive groves, or looked whimsically out on the sea by the cove. The journey had changed them, and that change had brought with it a new sense of identity. They were neither citizens, nor nomads.

Adrift, beneath transient stars.

When facing questions they had no answers for, the young used to turned to their elders. Their elders, in turn, used to looked to the skies, seeking constellations under the glow of the moon. Although even that now seemed wrong, after so much change: the traditions of the past no longer held sway. So, instead, both young and old turned to those who had guided them before. To conciliatory faces, and wise voices, who had helped them reach that distant place. There, as they had done before, they hoped to find their answers.

From the words of their own Prophet: now a young woman, and a mother too.

The young Prophet's journey had been one fraught with unease and moments of loss. She had guided her people from the walls of Arbash, fleeing an enemy of violent intents that had taken her own brother. She had led her people through the trials of seeking a new home, out on the desert sands, nearly losing her father in the process. She had brought them together, as one family, to settle New Arbash on the banks of the oasis. She had, for five years, fostered them as her own, rallying behind the hope that had carried them so far.

And the challenges had appeared unending, especially in those early days. After several flawed attempts at creating a new home, the people's hope had started to wane. Still, the young Prophet prevailed, both through desperation and a sense of faith. The Prophets that had come before, had come from nothing.

Now they, the former citizens, would have to do the same.

And so, after five years, New Arbash was lifted from the desert sands. Homes were built and stories were made within their sandstone walls. Families had been raised there; the young Prophet had had a daughter of her own. And in her tiny, inquisitive eyes, the Prophet could not help but see something of herself there: a mind forever questing, forever seeking the truth.

Wondering who they were, and what they would become.

I

HOME

I

As evening approached, and the pale blue skies became laced with ochre and gold, the vast oasis in the bowl of the dunes rippled with a delicate breeze, as if the waters were tossing and turning in some deep, gentle slumber. On the sandbanks ahead, the waves lapped at the shoreline. On the opposing side, palm trees swayed, and the reed-beds rustled like ancient instruments. The surface of the oasis, once a beautiful aquamarine, now lay dappled with silver and orange, producing a mirage like an old mirror, peering up at the stars.

Nights out in the Unknown were spectacles in of themselves. If one wrapped up to avoid the cold, they could peer up into the skies seemingly forever. The stars coated the dark like grains of sand; constellations depicted ancient stories and the whims of forgotten gods. There seemed not enough words in all the world to describe how bountiful it was up above. Much like the vastness of the Unknown, the night sky seemed to stretch on without end. Full of life, and full of secrets, under the watchful gaze of the moon.

And yet, sometimes, the small things were just as fascinating as the large: wading through the waters of the oasis then, a young girl traipsed about, her hands outstretched to hold her balance. She wore a pale blue dress with tiny ink spots like the spines of a cactus. Her wild hair, like a mane about her face, had been tamed into a loose bun atop her head. In the low light her eyes twinkled with curiosity, as her fingers tapped the water's surface, scattering the streaks of silver and orange. She followed the path of the ripples as they circled out from her touch, joining other waves to shimmer like scales. The oranges, flickering like fires, leapt and jostled for space. Mesmerised, she continued on her slow journey through the oasis shallows, giggling at the sudden splash of fish as they darted out of her path. With her eyes down, she never saw the beauty of the skies above.

But in many ways, she didn't need to.

She has found a beauty of her own.

Sat on the bank overlooking the oasis, My'ala let a smile form on her face, watching her daughter entertain herself wading through the shallows. She was in bliss; a world of her own. Part of My'ala wondered if she would be getting cold as dusk set, or if she would be happy walking home with wet feet.

She'll tell me if she does, My'ala decided, taking a long breath and smirking. At the thought, she was reminded of similar instances: including one just that morning, where her daughter had decided she didn't quite like her shoes and made a long speech explaining just why. My'ala had listened, and nodded, and smiled with a caring touch, watching the great wheels turn in her daughter's head, illustrating her beliefs. *She has quite the voice on her now. She knows her opinions. And she'll let you know them...* especially *when she wants something.*

"It still scares me, you know... looking at how fast she's grown."

Turning, My'ala looked into the pearly eyes of the God-Elect, Aurelius, who sat with his elbows on his knees, rolling a small pebble between his pale fingers. At his back, some distance away, his two guardsmen also stood vigil, facing away to give them some privacy as a family.

"She'll be three soon," Aurelius scoffed, smiling out to his daughter. "How the suns seem to pass so quickly..."

My'ala nodded. "I couldn't believe it when she started walking... and then her first words," she reminisced.

"Spoken with such confidence, too."

"She has so much spirit, so much *life* to her. She's a force of nature. It wouldn't surprise me if the sands bent around her feet when she walked."

Aurelius laughed. "If she doesn't get her own way, I don't imagine there's much that wouldn't move out of her path."

"Not if it had any sense."

"Or her mother wasn't watching..."

My'ala grinned, rolling her eyes at the God-Elect, before turning her attention back to her daughter out in the shallows. She was the little riot of My'ala's life; the blossom of beautiful trees. The fierce warrior and the charming lady. The diplomat, and the guilty thief. From the bearing of her when she was born, to the first words that left her lips, My'ala had been captivated by every little part of her. The tentative pawing of her hands; the open-mouthed wonder at every new type of food; the fascination with the footprints she left in the sand, trailing behind her like a shadow. My'ala and Aurelius had guided those footsteps around together, but in many ways she had guided herself: taking the world in both hands, carrying it on her tiny shoulders.

My little Ki'lu.

"I imagine she'll want to be heading home soon," the God-Elect said softly. "The flies that come out over the reed-beds will start to annoy her in a moment."

"Are you sure that's not just because *you* want to be heading home?" My'ala replied, lifting an eyebrow.

Looking to him, she watched Aurelius return the gesture. "There *may* be some truth in that, too."

In the low, ambient light, a certain maturity graced the God-Elect's face: one hewn from becoming a young father, and establishing life out on the sands. He had lost some of the softness that he had possessed living in the palace in Arbash. Thick lines ran along his brow, and around the contours of his eyes. He sported a small beard, kept short and neat, to provide a rugged appearance. The grain of his skin, especially across his cheeks, appeared coarse, almost like chalk. And yet, his eyes remained as blue and shiny as ever, like two twin gemstones locked in a beautiful mask.

They were reflections of just what kind of life he now lived – reflections that My'ala bore too, in her own, personalised way. Her skin had darkened under the sun's heat, and the birth of a child had added weight to her bones. Her joints creaked, and tenderness crept up her back and over her arms. Her hands, once so slight and smooth, now bore tiny scars and bruises from her journeys over the dunes.

But, despite that, her youthfulness still remained: her child-like wonder, as bold and strong as it had been before. It was a treasured thing; it was an act of defiance, especially in a landscape that was often so harsh and cruel. That, despite the speed of life, her mind still fell upon the quiet moments: curious, always, at the little details of the world.

A beauty of my own.

The padding of tiny feet drew My'ala's attention away from her thoughts. Turning her head, she saw Ki'lu racing up the sandbank towards her, her feet coated in a layer of sand. She wore a disgruntled look, a slight hint of frustration in her frown.

Someone's hungry, My'ala inferred, reaching out her arms to give her daughter a hug.

"What is it, my little gojan fruit?" she asked, brushing hair from Ki'lu's face.

"Home now… please," her daughter responded, tucking her arms in and tapping her fingers.

"Well, as you asked so politely, I'm sure we can do that. Are you cold at all? Hungry?"

Ki'lu nodded, looking between My'ala and Aurelius. From behind his back, the God-Elect retrieved a woven shawl and placed it around his daughter's shoulders, burying her in the soft cloth.

"That's better, isn't it?" Aurelius asked.

Ki'lu grinned, and then yawned. "Thank you, da."

"That's okay, little one." He lifted to a stand, brushing his robes of sand and small stones from the bank. "Come on then, let's get you home." He pointed up. "It looks like the sky will be very beautiful tonight."

Ki'lu giggled and squeezed her hands together. "But you say

that every day!" she exclaimed.

"And I mean it, too!"

"But you know what your da also says, don't you, Ki'lu?" My'ala added, taking Aurelius's hand as she got to her feet as well. "That the sky may be pretty, with all the stars and the lights in the world... but it will never be quite as pretty—"

"As *me!*" Ki'lu blurted.

The God-Elect smiled down at his daughter and ruffled her hair. "Exactly, Ki'lu. That's right. Never as beautiful as you."

Stepping alongside them both, My'ala took up her daughter's hand and guided her across the sandbank towards the village. With tiny, explorative steps, Ki'lu wobbled between her parents – taking a moment to look up to the stars, the glow of wonder in her eyes.

II

Nestled in the basin of the oasis, the settlement of New Arbash lined the outer ridge like a crescent moon, bathed in a warm light as dusk rolled over the dunes. Palm trees and dark green bushels dotted along the winding paths through the village. Single-storey block houses, like the teeth of a slumbering giant, dotted the earth around the sandbanks up to the water's edge. There, wooden pontoons extended out from slanting fishing huts, where small nets and spear-poles hung from pillars at their edges. Along the eastern ridge of the settlement, where the Unknown stretched unendingly to the horizon, tall guard-towers peered inquisitively out over the dunes, their stockades lined with cloth drapes to protect the guards from the sun. As darkness fell, the glow of torchlight dotted the village like lantern-bugs. Around fire-pits, villagers gathered to exchange food and sing songs.

To those same quiet melodies – accompanied by the tapping of leather drums – My'ala navigated the village perimeter with a sense of tranquillity and peace, approaching the wide portico of their home flanked by hibiscus bushes. It was a sprawling compound of three separate chambers, dotted with wooden beams and ornamental tiles, replicating the homes in Arbash but with a unique ruggedness they had lacked. The hibiscus bushes were awash with gold flowers and the buzz of insects; over the roof, tiny migrating birds darted through the alcoves.

"Someone's sleepy," the God-Elect commented, glancing down at their daughter. Hanging between them, Ki'lu's head lolled from side to side, her steps slow and ambling on the slope of sand.

"I think her cot may be calling," My'ala added – watching, for a moment, as Ki'lu's head lifted.

"No, ma..." she said, stifling a yawn as she spoke.

"Ah, my little hummingbird, look at you yawn! You can barely stand."

"No!" Ki'lu made to wave her arms, but found no strength to move her hands. "No, I... I'm *okay*..."

Shaking his head with a smile, Aurelius dipped his shoulders and scooped her up in his arms. Ki'lu, initially objecting, soon nestled into the God-Elect's collar, her hands clutching at the seam of his robe as if it were a cushion. She stirred there for a moment, cupped in her father's arms.

And within a heartbeat, she was quietly snoring, her mind away with the stars.

"*So stubborn,*" My'ala whispered, her face awash with oranges and blues.

"*I'd call it 'tenacious'*," Aurelius replied, smirking as they approached the front door.

Stepping ahead of him, My'ala gently shifted the lock and pushed the door open, allowing the God-Elect to step inside without disturbing Ki'lu. Her soft snores echoed in the chamber beyond, as My'ala stepped over the threshold behind them.

Within the house, soft candlelight illuminated the room with a delicate glow, crawling into shadowed corners like the questing buds of flowers. A dining table occupied the centre of the space, with folded drapes of dyed cloth separating the kitchen at the back. The table itself was an impressive slab of black stone, atop which sat platters and wicker mats threaded with reed-heads. Aromatic smells swam through the air around them: herbs and vo'zan meat, and the earthy sweetness of incense.

Two long, cushioned benches ran parallel to the table – and there, under the orange glint of the candles, three figures sat in conversation. Between them, steamed vegetables and flat-breads sat in delicate beige bowls. A large basin of stew had been divided between smaller dishes, garnished with salt-leaves from the marshes. The smell alone was enough to stir My'ala's appetite, but seeing the warm food in the actual bowls was almost impossible to resist.

"*I'll take her through to the cot, then I'll be back,*" the God-Elect whispered to her, circling the table towards the cloth drapes at the back. As he passed, he waved a silent greeting to those eating the stew, who in turn hushed their voices and nodded in reply.

My'ala smiled after him – her heart almost following him

through the house – before she turned to the long table and sat down, pulling her dress in about her legs.

Next to her, Su'la reached over and gave her a hug around the shoulders. "Good evening, sister," she said with a smile, the first lines of wrinkles forming at the corners of her eyes. Her hair sat wild and flowing about her cheeks, almost like a fire under the candle's glow. "It seems like a little someone is *rather* tired today."

"And still so stubborn," My'ala replied, shaking her head. "We were almost dragging her over the dune ridge to get here. Her head was on her chest."

"When did she fall asleep?"

"Almost as soon as Aurelius picked her up. I don't think I blinked and she was already away."

"Quite the little adventurer!" My'ala's mother said from opposite her, tearing another piece of flatbread from the bowl. The grey strands in her hair had blossomed to a flush of silver, with tiny jade earrings hanging from studs in her ears. "Did you take her out to the waters?"

"I did, yes," My'ala replied. "Her teacher in the learning chambers said that she did very well today, so I thought I would give her a little surprise as she doesn't have any lessons tomorrow. Did you know that she can name nearly every type of insect out in the oasis? Just from the shells?"

"She's a smart girl, very bright," My'ala's father mumbled, excusing himself with a mouthful of stew. He sat opposite Su'la, surrounded by larger candles to help with his poor eyes. The stern lines over his brow furrowed as he cleaned his lips, his tanned skin pulling taut like camel leather. "She should spend some time with her second-sister… apply this knowledge she's learning."

Su'la nodded, crunching through the stem of a leaf. "I would be more than happy to have her along, next time a research trip is planned," she replied. "Obviously not during an expedition into the dunes... but if we're ever in the marshes taking samples I can take her for the day."

My'ala smiled. "That would be lovely, thank you." Then she paused. "Providing there's nothing in there that could *harm* her at all..."

"She'll be safe, don't worry. We haven't found anything out there that would cause her harm." Su'la took a spoonful of broth, then held up her finger. "Apart from that one serpent we found... and that one you found in the storehouse, didn't you, da?"

Their father thought for a moment – a glossy reflection in his eyes – before he chuckled to himself and nodded. "Yes! Yes I recall," he exclaimed. "Scared the olives out of my colleague. We were checking the dried grains, and all of a sudden this little hiss came from between the stone slabs. You did well to get rid of that one, Su'la."

"Was it dangerous?" My'ala asked, thinking suddenly of Ki'lu, out on the waters by the reeds—

"No, it wasn't." Su'la placed a hand on My'ala's knee and squeezed it reassuringly. "We checked its fangs... there was no venom. Don't worry."

My'ala nodded, and let a breath fall between her lips.

"You mustn't worry so much, Mi-Mi," her mother said gently. "Ki'lu will be okay. She's a sensible girl, as much as she wants to run around the whole Unknown."

"It's not that, it's..." My'ala explained, before inhaling and adjusting her skirts.

"What is it, dear?"

My'ala swallowed and shrugged. "I grew up in a city with walls and towers. There was a guard on every street corner. Everywhere I went, I knew where I was and where I was going. It felt safe." She gestured towards the front door, and the wider oasis beyond. "Here, there are no walls. No towers, or guards on every corner. The oasis is safe, and the marshes are okay, but over that ridge... it's just *desert*. The Unknown. A place of heat and sand and biting flies. A place with hidden caves and tunnels with... who knows what down there. There's no protection from the sun, no other places for water..."

"A dangerous place," Su'la inferred.

My'ala nodded, picking at the vegetables and bread in front of her. "I was an adventurous child. I didn't leave the city limits until I was almost ten. Ki'lu is almost three... just as inquisitive as I was... but there *are* no city limits. The world she's growing up in... it's nothing like the one I did. There are the same people, true, and the same culture around her... but this is the *Unknown*. The thing we were always warned about."

"Parenthood is not something you can predict," her father consoled her, "regardless of where you are. You just make the best choices you can with what you have."

"But I don't know what I have, that's the problem," My'ala admitted.

I don't know who I am out here...

Reaching across the table, her mother held her hand, running her thumb over the ridges of her knuckle. "I can't tell you how to raise Ki'lu, Mi-Mi – only you and Aurelius can do that," she said softly, her voice honey-sweet and calm. "But as for not knowing what you have... well, you have us. All of us, here, and many more besides."

As she spoke, Su'la squeezed her knee again; diagonally,

My'ala looked across and saw her father smile.

"We will support you out here, as we have done these past five years, and give Ki'lu that same support," her mother continued. "We may not have the answers... but we can promise that you'll never face the *questions* alone."

My'ala smiled, and squeezed her mother's hand. Pulling away, she leaned her head against Su'la's shoulder. "Thank you all... I don't know what I'd do without you."

"You'd be a lot less wise," her father said with a smirk.

"And probably a lot more sane!" Su'la cackled, producing a laugh from the others around the table.

My'ala smiled, and felt her sister's heartbeat through the shirt of her collar. The rhythms of it soothed her, as she watched her parents gather more food from the bowls.

I am blessed, she thought, in a moment of reflection. *I am blessed by these people... and this life I have.*

Lifting her head, she dipped a piece of flatbread into her bowl of stew and tore it with her teeth. The vo'zan meat ground with the herbs; the oils coated her gums, the spices tingling on her tongue. She savoured the mouthful – the flavours and the senses – and let her mind ease slowly.

Ki'lu will be okay, she accepted, reaching for another dip. *She will be okay, and so will I. We're in this together. We have each other.*

She'll be just fine.

II

THE SAND-KING

I

The next day rose quietly, yawning open over the eastern ridge in a haze of red, ochre and blue. The light danced over the waters of the oasis; it scintillated over the palm leaves swaying atop their trunks. Passing between the houses of New Arbash, the bronzed faces of the inhabitants shone like metal shields, their eyes twinkling at the beauty of the Unknown that they called their home.

Dawn and dusk came and went almost in perfect harmony: awash with light, the skies were like an elegant painting by a master's hand. The colours blended like reams of cloth, flowing into one another without breaks. The smudges of distant clouds were chalky and thin, applied with the finest of brushes. The eddies of the dunes through the mid-ground, so numerous and vast, became suddenly impossible to define, as they met the edge of the horizon and merged as one.

From atop one of the guard towers, nestled on the western ridge of the settlement, My'ala looked back on the dawn sky with a sense of whimsy, admiring the light as it scattered over the rooftops of New Arbash. There was something magical about it, to her: as if it were a blessing that only they were allowed to enjoy.

A blessing to all of us, she acknowledged with a smile, the heat gently warming her face.

"It's one of the great honours of my work, watching this each morning," one of the guards said alongside her: a shorter woman with kind eyes and a bow tucked over her shoulder. She, too, had been looking out to the east, admiring the blossom of dawn. "There's no sight quite like it."

"It's amazing," My'ala agreed.

"I thought, after seeing the sun rise through the archway in the cove of Arbash, that no other dawn would match it... but I have no problem saying that I was completely wrong there."

For a heartbeat, My'ala recalled the walls of their former home – dwindling, slowly, as they moved deeper and deeper into the desert – and felt a pang of loss in her soul. She could also remember the sunrise through the archway in the cove. How the light glistened over the pastel pebbles and up the winding path to the city. The beauty and the peace of it, in the place they had once called home.

Where life was so different... where I was so different.

"You have the perfect vantage to view it from," My'ala commented, burying the thought with a long breath.

"We do!" the guard exclaimed. "And do you know what's the best thing about it?"

"Go on?"

"If you are up here when dawn breaks – just before the sun hits the horizon – something magical happens. Sometimes… only sometimes… you can see a flash of green out there, almost like a shooting star."

Listening, My'ala's lips curled up her cheeks, and a warmth filled her heart. "How… *remarkable*."

The guard nodded, then waved a hand. "Anyway, sorry, you came up here to look at our supplies… and I know you're busy, so I don't want to keep you waiting…"

"It's no bother at all." My'ala bowed her head to the guard, turning to their sacks and satchels. "I would never want to miss a nice sunrise, no matter where I am, so thank you for sharing it."

The woman grinned up to her, before stooping low to open the nearest cloth bag. "So, what did you want to take stock of? We have our arrows here, our sun-robes, an extra cover if the current one above us breaks." She gestured up to the sheet of cloth suspended from woven branches, which rippled softly with the breeze over the dunes.

"We're just after a stock of what you have, and what you've used since the last check," My'ala explained. "It's only to resupply you if you need it. My father can't move as well as he used to because of his chest, so I offered to come and check in his place."

"An immensely kind gesture. I hope Master Busskar is well."

"He's okay, he's just… he has trouble with coughs sometimes. The desert air has not been good to him."

The guard nodded. "Bless his soul. He deserves good health. I remember when he gave us extra rations when we had those bad sandstorms during the last dry season. Extra rations, and extra cloth strips for our mouths and eyes to block the sand.

I've always remembered that. I gave him my thanks."

"I never knew that," My'ala replied, lifting her brows. "That was very good of him. I imagine that was a really tough time for you all up in these towers."

The guard, laying their supplies out on the tower floor, took a break for a moment, recollecting the memory. "It was, I... I've never been in a place quite like it. To one day see all the way out to the Beyond... and in the next, to barely see past the ridge, with dust sealing your eyes together. We were up here for three days, having food and water winched up to us using rope. For a while I thought it would never end." She paused. "But I will tell you, when the sand finally fell, and the sun broke through the dust... that was a special moment. To finally see the horizon again, and the village still in one piece beneath us... that was a big relief."

"I can imagine."

"It gave us hope, you know," she added, returning to her work, "that if we could survive that, then we could survive anything. We faced the worst the desert could offer, and we made it through just fine."

My'ala – thinking on her conversation the previous day – swallowed and watched the guard unload the sacks. "And hopefully what we've done since then – with the window covers on the houses and the sand shovels in the stores – will mean that, when it happens again, we'll be more ready for it too."

"I certainly think so. We've already felt the benefits of it." Lifting her hand, the guard gestured to a roll of cloth lashed to one of the wicker poles above her. "That see-through cover there is the main example we have: it's been perfect when the winds have been high up here. It covers the whole west side of the tower, so I'm not here choking on sand."

"Have you seen many storms rising since the last dry season?" My'ala asked. "Obviously down below we never really see what's beyond the ridge…"

"We've seen a few – and had a few pass over us as well – but nothing quite to the scale of the ones from last season." Briefly, the guard looked over the lip of the tower wall – rising suddenly to her feet as she did so. "Ah! As you should mention it, it looks like one is brewing now…"

With a turn of the head, My'ala took a few tentative steps forward, her intrigue winning out against her caution. She had never seen the start of a sandstorm before, only its aftermath: the moment where everything was buried, and the *how* of it was often forgotten.

Following the guard's direction, she looked out over the yellow dunes and saw what had caught the woman's attention: a column of dust and sand, projecting up across the horizon. It was thick and swirling, like a phantom against the dark blues of the far sky. It grew and shifted, so she could almost trace it across the ridges.

"That's a massive plume," My'ala exclaimed.

"Ah, it's only a small one; they get a *lot* bigger than that," the guard replied.

"How much so?"

"Biggest ones are usually triple that size."

"And do they often move like that?"

Pausing, the woman frowned. "Like what?"

"Like… in one direction."

"I…" She stopped for a moment. "No… no they don't." Clasping the tower's outer wall, the guard narrowed her eyes. "I've never seen one move like that."

My'ala took in a breath, and felt her chest tighten slightly. There should have been nothing to panic her; there was nothing in what she saw that provoked any danger.

But if this guard doesn't know what it is... someone who's been watching the sands for years... then what could it possibly be?

"It seems to be circling around that outcrop over there," the guard said, extending a finger. "Maybe the rocks are distorting the wind, making it spiral?"

"Possibly," My'ala considered. "Have you seen it do that before?"

"I... no, no I haven't, admittedly. "

My'ala puzzled, assessing her options. If it was just the wind, she would want to clarify, just to give the all-clear and avoid any anxieties.

And if it turns out that it's something else... then I definitely need to go out there and find out. "How far out is that outcrop, would you say?"

"Not too far... maybe a few ridge-lines over."

"Have we scouted the area before?"

"I couldn't say for certain."

My'ala nodded, checking for her sword at her hip. "I'm going out there to investigate, then."

The guard turned to her, a mix of concern and confusion warping her face. "Are you sure about that? I mean... do you need someone else to go too? Like a guard or two? I would feel awful if you went out there and... you know, some harm came to you..."

"I'd rather not risk too many lives: I know the sands, so I should be okay," My'ala replied, turning to the long ladder that descended back to the ridge. Her heart trammelled in her chest; she briefly thought of Ki'lu. "All I ask is that the other guard towers and yourself watch the horizon for any signs of trouble. I'll try and stay in clear view for as long as I can. Use your lenses to signal me if you spot anything, and alert the God-Elect too."

"Yes of course," the guard replied, masking her hesitancy with a dutiful bow.

"Thank you." My'ala bowed her head, and turned onto the ladder. "I should be back soon. Just keep an eye out for me."

And offer any prayers you can spare, if it turns out to be more than just a spiral in the wind...

II

The rocky outcrop jutted from the sands like the knuckle of a giant's hand, protruding in several ridges before being swallowed by the dunes. Its basalt surface had been worn down by the constant erosion of the winds, revealing veins of black stone and columns of thick slate. Like ladders, the slate formed along the sides of the rock, where My'ala saw small insects and creatures shift in the meagre shadows. She imagined them using the structure as a home, sheltering when the heat grew too heavy – scurrying out when the moonlight fell, and the sands cooled beneath their feet. It was a behaviour that all creatures seemed to abide by in the Unknown: a tactic, researched by her sister, where animals could avoid the worst of the sun. In response, the settlers of New Arbash had done something similar, sheltering under their canopies when the heat became too much. Out on the dunes as she was then, My'ala wished she could do the same.

But duty calls, she mused, *and it is a call I cannot ignore.*

Pulling her head-wrap tighter about her hair, My'ala peered up into the skies overhead, the prickles of sweat forming under her eyes and across the lines of her brow. Having shed its dawn colours, the horizon ahead had swelled with blues and whites, contrasting the dull yellows of the desert that stretched on for leagues around. The temperature had risen as she crossed the dunes from the village, and the winds had abated with it. Looking ahead – navigating each peak and trough – it seemed like the sandstorm that had been growing had lost its vigour, too. What had appeared like a howling gale from the guard-tower, had become a gentle spout of dust.

Until, cresting the last ridge, it had ceased altogether.

How strange, My'ala thought.

Turning momentarily – retracing her footsteps over the dunes – My'ala lifted a hand towards the distant spire of the guard tower. After a few heartbeats, the glint of a signal lens flashed in her direction: two short bursts.

No danger. All clear.

She sighed with relief: not that she had anticipated danger, but the assurance was a welcome one.

And while I'm here, I may as well observe what I can from these rocks, she added. *Maybe this can be another spot to gather stone for building…*

On quick feet, angled to the side, My'ala descended towards the outcrop. The sand crackled underfoot, flowing through the ridges of her sandals. Ahead of her, beneath the awnings of the rock, small animals scattered into holes and caverns.

At its base, My'ala drew to a stop and pressed her hand against the slate columns, feeling the fragile substrate crumble beneath her touch. Without the sun's glaring heat, the surface still retained some of its coolness. She understood why the creatures sheltered there.

Some relief, in a place so devoid of it.

Around her, more sections of rock jutted from the sands, but were much more brown in colour. Hard nodules, almost like horns, pricked out from the sandy walls of the bowl. A clay-red earth appeared around the base of the outcrop, too, dotted with pits and grooves like the prints of camel hooves.

How has no-one ever researched this place? My'ala frowned, scanning the walls of the dune around her. *There's strange shapes everywhere. So many different materials. This could be fantastic for our settlement. We could build around the oasis; we could irrigate the sands. We could have actual crops again, not just whatever we can scavenge from the desert.*

Approaching a section of the dune on her left, she crouched down and observed a concentric formation in the rock. It was thick and crusted, like an old sea-shell.

I'll have to tell Su'la about this, and da. They need to know what's out here, so we can use it. And if it's this close to our settlement, without any danger, then that makes it even better—

Suddenly, a shudder went through the ground beneath her. My'ala bristled, noting a plume of dust pull up from the duneside on her left. Her immediate thought turned to the sandstorm.

Maybe it will still happen after all…

She adjusted her footing, and watched the dust plume settle back on the ridge. Blinking once, she then turned back to the circular grooves of the rock ahead—

And saw there an eye as big as a shield staring back at her, an entire world contained in the dark of its pupil.

Her mouth opened, but no sound exuded.

She stumbled away, tripping and landing on her back.

With scrabbling legs, she pushed herself towards the rocky outcrop behind her, sheltering beneath its hewn stone as she tried to control her breathing.

Opposite her, the huge eye blinked and studied her. Its amber iris, awash with yellows and greys, quivered and shifted in its socket.

For several moments, it remained there, blinking and watching. For several moments, My'ala clung to her robes, frozen in place with sweat streaming down her face. She could not move. She could not think. Breathing was an act of mercy—

When the eye abruptly closed, and the dune-side shifted.

And the entire desert seemed to spin before her.

From beneath the sands, scales emerged, tinged with rust and apricot under a stony-grey. A body, speckled with scars and iridescent streaks, pulled free of the clay-like earth. The spikes that had littered the ground at My'ala's feet, suddenly rose along the curve of a spine. The rock-face at her back trembled and showered her with dust, as a great veil of it rose skyward, clouding the blue and the white.

Time became inconsequential. The spiralling was endless, and dizzying. She could barely decipher what she was observing: the end and the beginning seemed to merge into one, until nothing made sense at all. My'ala mouthed quiet pleas, but no sounds emerged: not even a squeak of her fear would rise, trapped like the mouse she felt she had become.

Endlessly, the world span. The desert broke apart and reformed.

Until the huge, scaly body drew to a slow halt, encircling her and the rock she cowered against.

And from behind its mass, a giant head emerged, encased in

gold and bronze.

"*To whom do I owe... such a disturbance?*" the huge creature boomed: a percussive sound that trembled in My'ala's soul, and rattled through the bones in her legs. Within their mouth, huge white fangs emerged like steely knives; a long tongue, forked at the end, drew around scaly lips. Smoke pulled out from their nostrils, cresting the ridges that circled their vast eyes. Wisps of hair like sedge-grass sprouted from their chin, offering an almost-sagacious look. "*To what cause can one find themselves here, amidst my slumber?*"

Beneath its powerful gaze, My'ala swallowed and felt her stomach knot. Pulling out from beneath the outcrop, she steadied her voice. "I'm... I'm My'ala," she mumbled. "Who are you...?"

Slowly – eclipsing the light of the sun beyond – the massive creature lowered its head towards her, until she could almost reach out and touch the scaled edges of its lips.

"*I have gone by many names... in a life as old as the desert itself.*" The creature's breathing was low and thunderous. "*The Breach in the Dunes. The Storm-Soother. The Dragon Prophet of Old. So many names, all lost to time... so many stories to tell, little mouse.*" My'ala shuddered beneath them. With a snort of air, like two chimneys, smoke flushed from the creature's nose. "*But there is one name that I have always been known by... and it is one I intend to keep. I am Nehebu, the Sand-King... the last great beast of the Unknown.*"

Looking up to them – across the vastness of their body, woven in on itself like threads of cloth – My'ala tried to grasp the scale of the creature: the one that called themselves Nehebu, the Dragon Prophet of Old. She attempted to reconcile the age of the beast, studying its wispy hairs and the scars across its snake-like body. The scale of time, as well as size, that hung about them with such terrifying majesty. Creatures like the one she stood beneath were only ever known in stories; the first Prophets, settling Arbash long ago, had drawn such things around the walls of their palace. Giant, shelled monsters with hooked claws and barbs; winged beasts with many limbs, and long needles for mouths. They had been borne, so it was said, from the imaginations of storytellers, depicting ancient teachings for others to follow.

But, cowering beneath one as she did then, My'ala realised the fallacy of that belief.

They were all real... and now, it seems that only one remains.

"I... I don't understand," she said plainly, for lack of a better response. "Why are you here? What has brought you to this place, to... to our home?"

A rumble, like a furnace, and the creature Nehebu seemed to scoff at her. "*I am here... because that is where my passage has taken me,*" the Sand-King grumbled. "*The proximity to your settlement over the ridge... means nothing to me at all. You are a grain of sand, in the vastness of this desert... and were it not for this exchange, I would have never even seen you.*"

"So you aren't a threat to us?"

Another snort, accented by a ripple of amusement. "*Little mouse, if I were a threat... would I not have already eaten you?*"

My'ala swallowed with unease; she considered the sentiment and nodded. Shifting further out from beneath the rock, she dusted her robes off, never taking her eye from the Sand-King's huge jaws. "We thought there was a sandstorm growing out here, so I came to investigate," she said. "That's why I came out here and... and disturbed you."

The Sand-King shifted a wispy brow. "*If your intention was to walk* towards *a sandstorm... then you are more a fool than I have given your kind credit for.*"

"We noticed the winds were moving wrong. We thought it was to do with the rocks... I wanted to see for myself."

"*You are a spirited one,*" Nehebu exclaimed, narrowing their eyes. "*Were you not concerned... for your safety?*"

"I have endured much worse than a sandstorm."

"*Have you now?*"

My'ala gestured off towards the ridge behind her, and the guard-towers of New Arbash. "I was the one who brought all of those people to the oasis, over the deserts of the Unknown. I helped them build the settlement that you can see out there."

"*By your hand?*"

"Yes, it was... difficult."

"*And you did this all... alone?*"

"I..." A flash of jade crossed behind her eyelids; she envisaged a deep well in her mind, and the prickles of a thorny bush. "No, I... I did it with the help of a wise woman. Another Prophet, if you can believe it."

The belittling expression the Sand-King have given her shifted slightly, replaced by a look of intrigue. My'ala pulled at the hem of her breeches, dread rising in her chest.

"*By whom did you receive your guidance?*" the beast asked.

"A lady, called Othella the Muse. She... she joined us, and helped us find our home. Then she departed... she's with the stars now, I think."

My'ala watched the Sand-King above her, and noted the recollection in their huge eyes. It was only a flicker – a tiny candle in twilight – but nonetheless, she understood in that moment.

They aren't just here on happenstance...

"*Othella...*" Nehebu intoned, almost whimsically. "*That is a name I have not heard in a long time.*"

"She guided us to the oasis... she helped us decide to settle there, about five years ago," My'ala explained. "I... I miss her. She understood me."

"*She was always wise... and never forgotten.*"

"Did you know her?"

The Sand-King's tongue rolled over their lips. "*I did, many moons ago... she spoke to me of prophecy, and changing winds, before we parted ways.*"

"Do you... know what that means?"

"*I do not,*" Nehebu replied frankly. "*But what I will say, little mouse, is that I may have... underestimated you in this. For, if you have made acquaintance with Othella the Muse... then you have been gifted something few have ever known. And I do not believe this will be our last conversation, therefore.*"

Pieces fell into place in My'ala's mind, too fast for her to follow. "How so? Do you know of something? Did she tell you more, last you saw her? Is there a path I need to take, or something I need to do—"

"*In time, young one,*" Nehebu bellowed, warding off her questions. "*In time. There is much to consider... and something I must tell you of, first.*"

The dread and tension that had held her before tightened against her ribs again. "What is it?"

"*I do not usually interfere with the whims of mortals... being that your kind are foolish and petulant, straying too far from your paths,*" Nehebu explained. "*But in this moment, with the knowledge I now possess of you, I shall forgo my habitual reservations... and offer you a warning.*"

My'ala gulped. "A *warning*? About what?"

In response, the Sand-King said nothing. Their head, hanging for some moments, studied My'ala with a stony gaze.

Then, on her left, she saw the creature's vast body unravel itself slowly, the scales sliding over rock and sand where a mighty dune had once risen. In layers, the scaly skin pulled back, revealing more and more of the landscape beyond: the undulations of the sand, dancing off towards the distant guard-tower on the ridge.

Where lights were flashing from signal lenses. Three long flares.

Danger, danger.

My'ala gasped. "Are they warning about you?" she asked, scrabbling forwards to take a better look.

"*They are not occupied with us… they have not even noticed the change in the sands here,*" Nehebu replied. "*No, they are warning of something that has approached from the west. Something over the sands whence you came long ago…*"

At their words, My'ala's heart sank like a stone. *From the west…*

From Arbash.

The city of her home. The valley of her childhood. The place they had abandoned five years before, fleeing an unknown enemy with swords and ships.

Have they followed us out here? she thought, pulling her robes tight across her body. *Have they finally… after all these years…*

Oh, gods.

She turned to the Sand-King, watching the twitches of the scales around their jaw. "I have to go to them," My'ala announced. "If they're in danger, I—"

"*Then you must move with haste,*" Nehebu interrupted. "*Do not idle yourself here, like a long shadow.*"

My'ala nodded and scrabbled up the clay-coated rocks. "Will you be here when I return?"

"*I will permit you that, yes.*" The Dragon Prophet lowed their head. "*Now go... before it is too late.*"

Her heart thundered in her chest. Her mind spun in a thousand directions.

Clutching at the sword at her hip, My'ala turned and ran.

III

THE HEADMAN

Her legs burned, as she clambered up dune-sides and slid down their banks, scaling the sands like the summits of mountains, determination in her every stride. The heat was strong above, and the brightness of the world made her dizzy. Her breathing came in short bursts, like stoking a fire. Ahead, the solitary guard tower rose up against the ridge, its signal lens still and no longer issuing a warning. Whether that was because the danger had passed, or was close enough to see, My'ala did not know.

Clawing at the dunes with her hands, she scrabbled up another rise and skirted the edge of the village.

No sounds of distress rose from the houses beyond the ridge. No cries of fear, or pain. Panic eased in her heart, but My'ala's mind still ran through memories and fears. Of the long-boats in the sea, arriving at the cove beneath Arbash; the torches, and the coats of metal armour traipsing up the path; the dozens of tents over the pastel-coloured rocks, growing more numerous with each passing day. She imagined facing them, whoever they were: the strange newcomers from distant lands. Whatever danger faced the people of New Arbash then, had come from that same direction.

But it can't be them, she thought, although the doubt in her mind made the thought ring hollow. *They can't remember us. And even if they did, they must think we were long passed, lost to the wastes of the Unknown. Nothing survives out here.* She paused. *Although… we did.*

And if that can happen, despite the odds… then is there a chance that those same soldiers who came from the sea have found us now?

My'ala stumbled and slipped momentarily, the air hitching in her throat. An image of Ki'lu crossed behind her eyes, and made her want to cry. She was out there, somewhere, with her family and Aurelius. She was safe. She was okay.

But for how long? My'ala hissed.

I have to find them.

Having circled the northern edge of the settlement, My'ala clambered to the top of the ridge ahead of her to look out on the oasis below. On her left, the palm trees rose amongst the scrub at the edge of the marshland, concealing the fishing huts and outlying homes of New Arbash just beyond. Ahead of her, glistening radiantly, the oasis lay dappled with beautiful greens, washing gently against the sandbanks on the far side.

But on her right, out to the west, her eyes and her fears became suddenly acute: because there, around the outskirts of the basin, several dozen settlers had gathered. They formed a crescent around the ridge, clustered together like migratory birds. Their robes flushed in the wind, like sheafs of sedge-grass. Around the inner edge of their crescent, several of the village guards lingered with weapons in their hands – including the helms of the God-Elect's own, who stood at the centre with their spears primed.

What's happening over there? The scene was tense and foreboding. Descending the ridge ahead of her, beneath the glare of the sun, My'ala struggled to make out what was happening. At the northern banks of the oasis, she stopped for a moment and picked apart the shadows at the top of the ridge in the west.

To spy there a small cluster of figures, sat atop great camels.

Wearing armour, with swords at their hips, My'ala gasped.

Oh, no…

Circling the shiny body of water – pushing through the long grasses of the reed beds – My'ala resisted the urge to run, keeping her pace deliberate and measured. The humidity was heavy – made worse by the sweat that coated her skin – and the air in her lungs felt thin and useless.

She approached the outer clusters of the villagers and shifted through them, muttering apologies as she passed, desperate to get to the front. Their robes rustled as she passed; the heat of their bodies was terrific. Realising who it was, many of her fellow people stood aside to let her through, opening a narrow channel through the crowd where—

"*Aurelius,*" she breathed, spying his wave of blonde hair and the red streaks of his robes just ahead. Almost sensing her presence, he turned to her and offered the most fleeting of smiles – although it was soon covered by a stoic grimace that set her heart knocking in her chest.

What's wrong here? My'ala stepped clear of the crowds. *What's this all about—*

Reaching the God-Elect's side, she stopped in her tracks.

Her jaw clamped, and her entire body tensed up. Aurelius gave her a look of concern, as he turned back to the western ridge.

Where a man stood watching them closely, flanked by his guards, the sickly curl of a grin on his face.

Beneath a mobile canopy – held aloft by two shrivelled men in loincloths – the figure stood in a silver chest-plate with robes of the deepest blue. Ringed hands lay clasped against their back, so they stooped like a vulture. A flush of orange hair coiled atop their head, with large ears and a heavy brow that seemed to always frown. Their lips were thin, pursed like a mineral vein. Their eyes were deep, and watchful.

My'ala had never seen the man before. She had no idea who they were. After five years adrift in the Unknown, the sight of any other mortal made her uneasy – but something about the man before her sent cold shivers up her spine despite the heat. Something about their leering presence made her instinctively reach for her sword.

A man in robes, joined by servants and soldiers atop camels, My'ala deduced. *Clearly someone with authority.*

Or a great capacity for wrongdoing.

Opposite her, the robed figure grunted and cocked an eyebrow. "And who might you be?" they inquired, their voice mellow but firm. With their palm open, they gestured to the basin around them. "How strange, to find one such as you. Such a jewel… in such a *wasteland*."

"My name is My'ala," she replied, with strength and a fire in her throat. "And to whom am I speaking?"

The man flashed his teeth and nodded. "It is good to meet you, My'ala." He clicked his tongue. "And out of respect, I shall honour your question with an answer of my own. I am the Headsman of my people. I have led them across this vast world, and let them prosper. I am the one they abide by, and the one who rules..." Lowering his arm, he produced a mock bow. "But you... may call me *Nero*."

The name sent a shudder through the village guards nearby. My'ala whispered it, and it tasted bitter on her tongue. Even the servants, adjacent to their supposed-ruler, seemed to cower away when he spoke.

What kind of man is this?

"You said your people have travelled across this desert," My'ala inferred. "So from where did you come from, to end up here?"

"We are travellers – nomads, if you will – from distant places," the man called Nero explained. "We hail from the hills in the south, where the rocks meet the sea. We hail from the long, slow river of reeds that marks its estuary. We are from the numerous towns along the seaboard, that we pass between in our ships. There is nowhere we have not been... there is nothing we have not made our *own*."

"How can you claim ownership of rocks and sand?"

"Because we build, and we grow. We take what we are given... and take even *more* that we're not—"

"And what of Arbash?" Aurelius interjected, receiving a scowl from the Headman for the interruption. "The city, due west of here... do you know of it?"

"Know of it?" A cackle escaped his thin lips. "My, what you don't know! That is my crown jewel. The greatest holding we possess in all our realm! With its clementine groves and its beautiful stone streets. It was such fortune that we came across it, all those years ago..." A sly smile spurned on his face. "...with the gates left open for us, by those *weak* enough to abandon it."

The God-Elect grunted. "We had no choice."

"Ah, so it *was* your people." The man called Nero tutted. "And to think, it was such a shame that you ran away before we could get to *know* each other."

"It was an eviction, on fear of death," My'ala hissed, her anger suddenly flaring. She was reminded Arbash's fading walls as their caravan had gone into the Unknown: the bronze minarets peaking over the sands, before they were swallowed by the haze of the sun. It had been a sorrow for her for a long time, revisiting the image – a sorrow made even more acute, realising what kind of people had since occupied it.

"There was no eviction," Nero chastised. "You left of your own accord."

"And you would have acted peaceably, had we stayed?"

"On the whole." His face hardened. "You would become our subjects... another addition to our seaboard realm."

"*Subjects?*" My'ala scoffed. "With swords and shields brought against us? We would have been *slaves*. You made that point when you killed our defenders..."

My brother, she thought, with a pinch in her heart.

"We brought metal against metal: if your intention was to drive us back into the sea, then our response was to do no such thing." The words came out as a growl; Nero wiped spittle from his chin. "And now, your former city is ours... and we rule it as we *wish*."

"Then you have won all you need to, surely?" Aurelius exclaimed. "You have your city, your '*prize*' as you call it... why come all the way out here, to us? The Unknown is vast. We have no quarrels with you."

The Headman wagged a finger. "Ah, but I have a quarrel with *you,* God-Elect. You, and all of your people here. Because

I know you came from that city… and I know, out here, you have built anew."

"We mind our own, it's true. We have built this place. But we mean no harm to you or your people—"

"Ah, but that is not true!" Nero snapped. "That makes you a rival: another people, out here to *usurp* me. You may have plans to reclaim this Arbash you speak of. To raise an army, one day, and march on my crown jewel. And I cannot have that. No, I will *not* have that…"

"That is not our plan," My'ala said with certainty. "We are not that way."

"*Everyone* is that way. Do not think you are so special."

"*We* are not that way. Look, I don't know by whose teeth you have been bitten before, but… please, we are just settlers out here. We're just trying to survive, that's all."

"That may be so… and if all you're doing is surviving out here, then we shall never have any means to fight. But if that *is* your intention, then there will also be no harm in you '*surviving*' under the banner of the Headman, where I can maintain control and have my soldiers keep an eye on you."

"We do not accept your terms," Aurelius commanded. "We are free, and we shall remain that way."

The Headman pursed his thin lips, shaking his head slowly. "I was afraid you would say that. Such is the folly before the fall…"

"What are your intentions with us?" My'ala asked, her hand never leaving the sword-hilt tucked away under her robes.

"My *intentions*? My intentions are simple enough: if you do not bow to me with a turn of the head, then you shall bow to me at the end of a *sword*."

"We will fight you, then." Behind her, My'ala found strength in the rattle of her guards' armour. "We shall push you back to Arbash, if we have to."

Around the Headman, his servants and guards seemed taken aback by her words. Her defiance came like a punch to them, catching them off-guard. But the man called Nero, at the centre of them all, remained stone-faced and unperturbed.

Until a smile cracked open on his face, and he turned to the side.

"My'ala – that is your name, yes? – please, come with me, just to the top of this ridge," Nero requested. "You shall not be harmed, I promise – such would be a waste of such a desert gem as yourself. No, rather, I have something to *show* you..."

With a wave of his hand, the Headman told his guards to move back, opening a channel through the middle for My'ala to ascend.

My'ala, watching the man meander his way up the slope beneath his canopy, glanced to the God-Elect briefly, unsure of whether to follow.

"*We're right here,*" he whispered to her. "*Keep your distance... see what he wants.*"

Taking a long breath, My'ala stepped forward and followed the Headman up the ridge, stopping alongside him at its peak to study his porcelain features.

"What is it?" she said plainly, aware of the guards at her back.

"A fight... that's what you wanted, is it not?" Nero inquired, before slowly raising a hand to point at the horizon. "Then, if you wish to engage in such folly... may I present to you, your subsequent *fall*..."

My'ala followed the Headman's direction – out across the dunes and the rolling sands – until, at the midground of the horizon, she saw a shape looming out of the desert—

And felt her stomach knot with fear.

There was a camp out there, on the sands. A dark smudge on the horizon. Pillared tents, in an area three times the size of their village. Against a pale sky, columns of smoke rose from cooking fires. The tiny dots of people passed along the verges, likely armed with a blade or a bow each. She had no idea on the number of souls dwelling beneath the canopies.

More than we have, she admitted. *Far, far more...*

The thought curdled in her chest. Her head thrummed with pain. She thought of everything behind her – the houses and the people who had made the desert their home – against the might of the camp sprawled out in the distance.

She thought of the soldiers flooding out from beneath the canopies. A tide, swelling through the streets of New Arbash, swords glinting in their hands. My'ala shuddered at the thought; the idea of defending against them curdled in her gut.

It cannot be done, she pleaded, all the strength gone from her legs. *It cannot be done... we cannot challenge something like that.*

"Remarkable, is it not?" Nero mused, watching her face sour. "I certainly think it is. They are all my people – largely soldiers and servants – who have joined me on this little journey to your home." He leaned in closer to her; My'ala remained frozen. "It scares you, does it not? To see all of that, out there, awaiting my command. I could tell them to march, you know? I could tell them to come to me now, to occupy this little settlement of yours. We would look after most of you... *most* of you. I would be lenient, of that you can be sure." He paused, his eyes flickering. "But, rather than that, I want to make a deal with you, young My'ala... one that I don't think, in the circumstances, you will be able to refuse."

My'ala swallowed bile, and held her jaw tight. "What?" she

asked.

"I will give you three days. Three days, where no harm or harassment will come to your people. And in those three days... I want you to find a reason why I *shouldn't* annex your little home here. *Convince* me of why I should just leave you be, and never come back. Tell me who you are, and what you stand for, and if the reason is good enough, I will go..." He paused, leering forward. "But if you don't, I will send my army here to you... and you better *pray* I'm in a good mood."

My'ala blinked, her mind racing, her body frozen with nerves.

A reason, she breathed. *A reason why we should be here. We, the people, dispossessed of our home and forced to live in the desert. Answering the question: who are we, and what does our future hold?*

She sighed quietly, rolling her tongue.

Where would I even begin...

"You have three days, starting from now," Nero announced. With a flick of his hand, he summoned his guards, who crested the dune ridge and began their departure down the other side. "On the third day, I shall return here, and hear what you have to say. If it is worthy, we shall go... if it is not, expect my army to follow." He grinned, before turning away. "Good luck to you, *My'ala.*"

Ambling down the dune, with his sprawling camp in the distance, My'ala watched the Headman depart with his canopy-bearing servants in tow. His remained stooped and studious; lifting a sleeve, he wiped spittle from his mouth again, sniffing and clicking his tongue.

At My'ala's back, watching Nero's departure, the guards rallied to the crest of the ridge – stopping to look in horror at the horizon, their swords hanging limply in their hands.

Behind them, gasps issued from the gathered crowds. Young and old wept, consoled by others grappling with their fate and hope. It was a hope that had guided them from the gates of Arbash, and across the deserts of the Unknown. It was a hope that had helped them for five long years around the oasis of their new home. It was a hope that had served them as a family, unified as one whole.

And now that well is almost dry, My'ala mourned, *when faced with odds such as this.*

She thought of her mother and father, and Su'la. She thought of Ki'lu, young and so innocent, cradled in her arms. All the people she had protected; all the people she loved.

Their lives now in danger. Their way of life now put to ransom.

From alongside her, Aurelius stepped in and wrapped his hands around her arm. His presence was comforting; his scent faint but relieving. "I'm so sorry, My'ala," he said softly, his expression forlorn. "I truly don't know what to say."

"I don't know either," My'ala admitted, her throat in a tangled knot.

"I'm not sure what to suggest, either. What do you think we should do from here?"

With an intake of breath, My'ala's mind spun, trying to grapple onto ideas. Her legs were numb, and in a malaise she struggled to remain upright. In her mind, she searched and searched, her vision blurring and fading with adrenaline – until one such idea came to her, in the very back of her head, rising to the fore all of a sudden.

Prophets led me from Arbash… Prophets led me here, she thought.

And perhaps a new Prophet can save us all from being servants to that madman too.

"Gather the people and give them extra rations; no one

works today," My'ala decided. She turned to Aurelius, staring deep into the blue of his eyes. "Give them comfort, and remind them of the odds they've survived before. We need that hope more than ever now."

"Okay... and where are you going?" he asked.

"I have to see someone... out in the desert. They can offer guidance, like Othella, and I ... I need you to trust me, please." Without explanation, she planted a kiss on his lips: they were soft and warm, like a fresh fruit. "Protect everyone. Give them comfort while I'm gone. You have to trust me."

Aurelius hesitated for a moment, caught between his fear and his stoicism. But, after a heartbeat, he nodded and exhaled. "You have my word, My'ala."

"Thank you, Aurelius." She gave him another kiss, before turning out to the sands in the east. She checked her sword at her hip, and adjusted her sandals against the grain of the sand.

Time to go and find this Sand-King again, she thought, *and pray they have answers I can use...*

IV

THE ULTIMATUM

She found Nehebu in a deep slumber, nestled against the same stone outcrop where she had disturbed them last time. They had not bothered to conceal themselves – she imagined it was a rather tedious process – but instead lay coiled like a sunning snake with their nostrils streaming smoke, woven into the dunes in long, broad waves. With how still they were, My'ala almost believed that they were some ancient statue, built by a lost civilisation and uncovered by the winds. The scales could have been carved; the rings around their eyes could have been etched. As she approached, the sense of time seemed to press in against her.

"Sand-King!" she cried out, stumbling down a dune slope. "I must speak with you."

From over the undulations of their body, she saw the Dragon Prophet's eye slide open gently at her call. A long rasp of breath sent a plume of sand up into the air. Their head shifted, and turned towards her.

"*We must find other means of talking... these disturbances are not pleasant,*" Nehebu grumbled, lifting their massive head from the rocks. As they moved, a guttural sound burst from their throat, rippling over their jaw and down their tongue as it extended from their lips. My'ala wondered if it was frustration, or some challenge of their kind – before she realised the Sand-King had actually just yawned. "*What must you speak of, little mouse?*"

"The danger they alerted us to, to the west of our village, I..." she muttered, struggling for words. "I was right. There were travellers from Arbash, my former home, and they... I spoke to someone, and... there's an army out there, Sand-King. A huge mass of tents. They all have swords and bows, and are ruled over by this Headman of theirs. We met with them, and they spoke to us, and I..."

I'm scared, she longed to say, but held her tongue in the presence of the beast. *I'm scared, and I don't know what to do.*

Nehebu listened, and waited. With a narrowing of their orange, orb-like eyes, they then turned to the distant west and studied the horizon there. The smoke continued to billow from their nostrils. The lines tightened on their features, detailing the extent of their thoughts. But it wasn't confusion that My'ala saw there – it was almost the opposite.

It's familiarity, she noted, suddenly concerned. "You know who they are... don't you?" she asked.

"*They are known to me,*" Nehebu explained. "*I have encountered their kind before. They are, as you say, travellers of this great Beyond. Travellers... but also conquerors.*" The Sand-King looked down to her. "*Tell me, what did they say to you?*"

"That we are a threat to them, out here. That we... because

we once lived in the city they now covet as their own, they cannot trust that we will not try and return one day, and take it back."

"*And would you, given the chance?*"

My'ala paused. She hadn't even considered the possibility of returning to Arbash one day, let alone the scale it would take to reclaim it. "I... no, I don't think so. I genuinely don't know."

"*Hm.*" Nehebu worked their jaw. "*That answer would not satisfy their appetites, I fear. What were their terms?*"

"Their terms?"

"*What are their intentions? What do they* want? *You still live and so do your people. And as you are not currently among your kin, preparing your defences, I can also assume that they do not intend to attack your settlement this very moment.*"

"No, no, they... their Headman – a man called Nero – he gave me a chance to save my people, and to stop us becoming more of his '*servants*', as he called it." She recounted the conversation. "He said we had three days, including this day, to find an answer to a question for him. And if the answer was good enough, he would leave and never return..."

"*And what was this question?*"

"Why we deserve to be here," My'ala said morbidly. "Who we are, and what our future holds in this place."

Above her – hanging like the boughs of an ancient tree – Nehebu snorted and licked their teeth. "*There are no easy answers to a question of that size,*" they boomed. "*Especially when confronted with a man such as he...*"

"What do you know of them?"

"*I have seen this happen before, in the south where the river lies: the same tented city you speak of, decamped just beyond the border of a* desert town by the waters. They were similarly left for several days, to consider answers to questions they could not know. Meanwhile, this Nero waited and watched from afar."

My'ala frowned. "What happened to them?"

"They tried at first to reach an answer, but soon went mad with the stress. There was infighting, and fires within the walls of the town. Some of them stayed and tried to put up defences, hoping to block the invaders' path." They paused. "But many tried their luck crossing the huge river... and met their fates beneath its swell."

A shiver ran down My'ala's neck, in spite of the heat. She had sensed something wicked in the way Nero had spoken to her, but with the Sand-King's story, that wickedness seemed to be more like madness.

And where could we go, if left to the same fate? We have no river to cross, no walls to defend. We just have the desert – more and more of the Unknown – and they have an entire army, that could catch us without fuss ...

"We're doomed then," she said aloud, not realising at first that she had spoken. "We have no way of defending ourselves..."

"Unless you hold the Headman to his word, and find an answer to satisfy his question," Nehebu retorted. Tilting their massive head, they gazed down at My'ala, the hairs along their jawbone waving in the wind. "*Those in the town by the river fell apart when faced with such a task... but you, with the wisdom you have garnered so far in life... you may find answers where they could not.*"

"But how?" Unease punctured her words. "I don't know who we are. We aren't citizens. We aren't travellers. We don't *have* the answers. I don't know what our future holds... how can I, when we only focus on surviving day by day?"

"*Then perhaps that is where you should begin: the* why *of your survival.*"

"I don't have that answer," My'ala sighed. "We were forced from our homes, and we've made new homes out here. We scavenge for food, grow crops where we can, and use what we can find to build our dwellings. Our focus is living out here, not *why* we're living at all…"

"A dwelling is not built without a cornerstone. A fishing hut is not built without fish to catch. A well is not dug, if not for the water down below. Hope may let you achieve these things, and family may give you cause to do them. But why do anything, if at first you have not understood what it means to 'do' at all?"

My'ala rubbed at the bridge of her nose, and hissed. It was all too much: worrying about her family, and the actions of the army camped beyond their border ridge. The question she had been given by the Headman, of who they were and why they deserved to live in freedom. The teachings of Artemis and Othella, blending into one in her mind. It consumed her; like an eclipse, it covered over her other thoughts. Above her, the Dragon Prophet loomed large and sagacious.

Guided here by hope… held together as family. She breathed in, and out, and in again. *Now, we have to answer why we have done any of it at all: not our purpose in life, but who we are at its core.*

"I don't know," she said meekly. "I don't know what that means."

Nehebu nodded. *"And it will take time."*

"Time that we don't have."

"Regardless, I see in you a strength and a determination," the Sand-King expressed. *"And because of that, in the face of such torment, I shall offer you something."*

"What is it?"

"I shall be your guide, little mouse. Should you find answers, return

to me, and I shall inquire upon them. I do not usually act in the affairs of small mortals... but on this, I believe I can make an exception." They paused. "*Just do not fall below my expectations.*"

My'ala bowed her head, both with a sense of relief and an eddying wave of fear. She had prayed that the Sand-King would help her in her cause, and formulate some answers to her questions.

But at what cost? she wondered, biting her tongue. *What expectations do they have of me, that I may fall beneath?*

"Thank you, Nehebu," she replied.

"*Do not worry yourself on giving thanks, little mouse... I am far too old for such things,*" the Sand-King replied coyly. "*Now, scurry back to your people: be with them, and learn what you can. Sometimes the minds of others can open yours in ways you did not expect.*"

Turning from them, My'ala pulled her robes tighter about her body and squinted against the glare of the sun. Her head span, her thoughts orbiting a central wont to find answers and keep her people safe. Despite the gravity of her situation, she still held out hope that an answer would be found somewhere.

I just have to think, she proclaimed to herself. *I just have to think, and pray.*

At her back, the Sand-King twisted back into their coils and lay their head down next to the outcrop. Within moments, she watched their eyes close, and the draw of sleep take hold once more.

"*I'll be back,*" she whispered, watching the smoke pull from their nostrils, scaling into the blue sky like thin threads of cloth.

My'ala returned home to find Aurelius waiting for her, sat in

Ki'lu's bed-chamber as the little girl snored softly. In her palm-framed cot, she nestled into the straw pillows and pawed at the mattress beneath her, the room dimly lit from small windows on the back wall.

On her entrance, the God-Elect got to his feet and wrapped My'ala in his arms. My'ala, in turn, seemed to crumple into him, resting her head against the bone of his collar. Her legs shook from exhaustion, and tears threatened in her eyes. Peering past him, the sleeping shape of her daughter brought a fearful heat to her heart.

"Are you okay?" Aurelius asked, stepping back and holding her hands. "What happened? Where did you go?"

"I'm not sure of what you'll make of my answer," My'ala mumbled.

The God-Elect shrugged. "Try me."

"I went out to the north-west, to an outcrop between the dunes. There's a creature out there... an ancient beast. They are called the Sand-King."

"A *creature*? Like... what?"

"Like the creatures from the old stories. The tapestries in the old palace in Arbash."

"I thought they were just stories..."

"It turns out that they aren't. I found one. Their name is Nehebu, and they're this massive dragon-serpent creature, and... and they knew who *Othella* was, Aurelius."

"As in, the lady from the well, who helped us get here?"

"Yes, her. They've encountered each other before. It's why... it's why this Sand-King is here at all, and agreed to speak with me. Because when they heard about the Headman and the camp they offered to help us – or to help *me*, rather, in finding answers, but... but I don't know what they mean, or what they're looking for..." My'ala closed her eyes and hung her head. "This is just all so *much*..."

"Hang on, slow down." Aurelius squeezed her hand, centring her. "First of all, is this... *Sand-King*, or whoever they are, a threat at all? Do we need to monitor them? Are they planning to stay clear of the village?"

"They won't harm us," My'ala confirmed, her eyes glassy like the surface of the oasis. "They will stay away... they're only here long enough to help us. Really they have no interest in us at all: had I not found them yesterday, they probably would have just passed us by."

"And you're sure of that?"

"I think so."

Aurelius nodded. "Okay, that's good. And this help they want to provide for three days... that's to do with the Headman's question, yes?"

"They want to give us a chance... they know of this Headman, and what they're like."

"And will they give you an answer *themselves*? If they are as ancient as they claim to be, I imagine they would have a lot of knowledge about it..."

"I don't think so, they..." She sighed. "No, they won't. They will help, but they won't interfere."

"Okay... okay, I understand." Aurelius met her eyes. "And how has that all left *you* feeling, My'ala? Not worrying about anyone else at the moment... how are *you?*"

At his words, she wanted to cry. She wanted to go out and face them head on. She wanted to cradle Ki'lu, hide away in some dark space and pray it was all a dream.

But I cannot do that... I have a duty to these people, and their safety, she admitted. *I brought them out here... I helped to settle this place. I can't abandon them now.*

As hard as this is going to be...

"It's left me shaken," she said, "but determined too. If we need an answer for Nero, then that must be our focus, regardless of how I feel. I don't want everyone to be involved" – she thought of Nehebu's story, and the infighting in the town – "but we need to be able to rely on each other nonetheless. We need to stay strong, and prepare for the worst, while I try and work out this answer."

"My'ala, you don't have to take all of that weight on your shoulders," Aurelius acknowledged. "That's not fair on you..."

"I'm not, don't worry. I have the Sand-King, and you, and my family... that's all I've ever needed."

Pulling in close, she hugged him again, before turning to brush the hair from Ki'lu's sleeping face.

"Your strength amazes me, you know that?" The God-Elect put a hand on My'ala's back.

"I just want everyone to be happy and safe." My'ala stood tall, and looked over his sand-grain features. "If that means I take on more of the decisions, then that's what I'll do. These people deserve a chance, and I – with the help of Nehebu – intend to do just that."

"You make me proud, My'ala... proud of you as a woman, and as a mother." Leaning in, Aurelius kissed her cheek. "And whatever you need, I am here with you every step. Never forget that."

"I won't," My'ala replied, finding calm in the rounds of his eyes. "Thank you."

"You're welcome." The God-Elect smiled – then, a flash of memory caught their face. "And also, before I forget, your sister mentioned something about you earlier. She made an offer... before she went out with her research team."

"Oh did she?" My'ala rolled her eyes. "I thought I told everyone not to work today?"

"I *tried* to tell her." Aurelius shrugged. "But you know what she's like."

"What was the offer, anyway?"

"She asked if you wanted to go with her to the mouse burrows in the south tomorrow morning and collect some eggs. I think she knew this whole situation would stress you out, so wanted to give you some time away to think and focus on something else."

For a moment, My'ala paused and considered. With her mind spun like a loom, the idea of finding mouse dens seemed a very welcome distraction. "I think that would be good... a nice distraction like you said." Then she paused. "Would... would Ki'lu be okay, do you think? If I went out for a few hours? I know she doesn't know what's going on, but..."

Aurelius shook his head. "Ki'lu will be fine, My'ala," he said gently. "Go and be with your sister tomorrow. Find some eggs. I'll keep an eye on Ki'lu here. Don't worry."

My'ala nodded, smiling at his smooth confidence. "I... you're right."

"I know I am." He winked, then stepped forward and pecked a kiss on her cheek. "We just have to take each moment as it comes with this. Keep our focus where we can. Use today as you need, and face tomorrow with strength."

My'ala nodded, glancing down at her daughter's sleeping body.

Keep our focus where we can, she repeated. *Take each moment as it comes.*

And pray those moments bring us closer to the answers that we need.

V

INNOVATION

The following day...

Ducking low to the sand, Su'la ran her fingers over several coarse lines on the dune-side, divining some tiny detail therein that My'ala had no knowledge of. Having followed her sister out over the wave-like bends of the Unknown that morning — skimming down ridges and scrabbling up dunes as big as mountains — My'ala was amazed by how freely her sister could navigate the terrain. She adjusted her footing like a dancer, measuring her balance like a spear-fisher. Every motion was deliberate, and never once did she seem close to falling over. Through the previous five years, she had honed her skills not only as a researcher of the wilds, but also as a sand-walker. The Unknown had become Su'la's proving ground.

And My'ala couldn't help but watch in amazement.

"The burrows are nearby," Su'la informed her, scanning the length of the dune-side ahead of them.

"How can you know?" My'ala asked, pulling her robes tighter about her head as a gust of wind swept up from below.

"Come closer, I'll show you."

My'ala stepped in and bent down next to her, trying not to disturb the striations in the sand. "What is it?"

"So these thin lines" – Su'la pointed at grooves along the crest of the dune beneath them, then followed them down the length of the ridge ahead – "they are from the sand-mice's wings. When they find a suitable path over the dunes – or to somewhere with water, or food – they will trail their wings behind them to let others know of the path. That way, none of them get lost, or fall prey to falcons or snakes. And, because these lines here are thicker, that means they've been used quite recently – otherwise, the winds would have buried them already."

"I see." My'ala nodded, imagining the tiny creatures dragging their thin wings behind them. "And these mice... how far do they usually travel?"

"Only a few hundred feet in any given direction, or until they find a water source normally. As you can imagine, water guides a lot of animals' movements out here."

"And with their burrows, do they just dig into the dunes?"

"No, the sand moves too much for them to do that." Su'la lifted to a stand. "I imagine, somewhere down the ridge ahead of us, we'll find a little patch of compact ground between the dunes where they've built their dens. They need solid earth to keep their tunnels open, otherwise they'll collapse." She smiled, offering My'ala a hand. "So... shall we go and find them?"

My'ala returned the smile and clasped her hand, lifting back onto unsteady feet. "Lead the way, sister."

Navigating the dunes once more, they followed the path of the sand-mice along the ridge, shielding their eyes from the glare of the sun as it rose overhead. It was still early in the day, with the worst of the heat yet to come; a low wind pulling across from the east was a relief to My'ala's body. But that factor – along with the heat – was at the back of My'ala's mind as she followed her sister. The lingering doubts about the Headman's question rendered everything else obsolete. The exchange they had had beneath his canopy repeated in her head over and over again, and despite the welcome distraction of finding the mouse burrows, it could never make My'ala forget the danger in Nero's parting words. She had spent much of the previous day embroiled in such thoughts – while helping others prepare their stockpiles and giving reassurances to the elderly – but despite that, she still found herself at a loss for any answers to his question.

Because, as Nehebu said, how can you answer a question so vast? she thought. And, to make matters worse, My'ala knew her fears were not just mental: for, if she looked too far to the west, she could even from a distance make out the tiny canopies of the soldier camp beyond. A place where swords were being sharpened; where armour was being polished.

No doubt the Headman is out there, rubbing his hands together, awaiting our defeat. As if he's just going through the motions, before the inevitable. My'ala scowled, before supressing her bitterness with a sigh. *But that isn't important. That can't be what we spend these days worrying about. We can only focus on ourselves, and what the people need: leadership, and answers. One of those I can provide, and will always provide. The other...*

She sighed again.

"There are the burrows!" Su'la exclaimed, pointing down the dune-side as it fell away beneath them.

Following her direction, My'ala spotted a patch of orange-coloured earth at the trough between the sands. Littered with small stones, it was hard to distinguish anything against the brightness of the sun – but, as she drew closer, My'ala saw tiny holes dotting the clay, and understood what her sister meant.

"They dig them diagonally to avoid the worst of the wind," Su'la explained, reaching the base of the dune and helping her sister down. "Because of how thick the earth is, it forms this little cap over the entrance to stop them being covered over."

"But what happens when the wind moves the dunes?" My'ala asked, wiping sweat from her brow. "This area will be covered again in a few days. Won't they get buried?"

"I'm glad you asked that." Su'la gave a knowing grin, pointing to two of the holes several feet apart from each other. "They're very smart, these mice. From which way does the wind blows the most out here, would you say?"

"From the east, out in the Unknown," My'ala replied.

"Agreed. And what do you notice about the holes beneath us?"

For a moment, My'ala studied them, frowning. "They... are also going in that direction. One to the east, and one slightly west of that..." She paused, considering, then locked eyes with her sister. "Are they... part of the same burrow?"

"Very good." Su'la nodded, crouching down to observe them more closely. "Every burrow has two openings: a main one, and an emergency one. The mice use their wings to determine in which direction the wind blows the most, then dig out the second opening based on that. That way, if they have a really bad sandstorm overnight, and the dune covers the main entrance, they can still escape to the surface by another route." She pointed to the hole further to the east. "In fact, I imagine that hole on the far side was once an emergency opening to another one that's now buried. And that one, to another, and so on…"

"So you're saying that, beneath the dunes… are loads of tiny interconnected burrows, which have been dug and then buried hundreds of times?"

"Hundreds, if not thousands, yes." From her waistband, Su'la unhooked a wide, hollow pipe of reed. At one end, it had tiny metal barbs, almost like claws. My'ala had seen it when they had first set out, and was still curious as to its function. "The only time the mice will move from their line of burrows is if the compact ground runs out: then, they'll gather their pack, and go out in search of somewhere new."

"Like we did," My'ala mused, scoffing with surprise. *Perhaps we are not so unlike these animals after all.*

"Exactly so." Her sister reached over and squeezed her arm, almost sensing the unease My'ala felt. "And they survive against all sorts out here in the desert… so think of how much we can survive and overcome too."

My'ala nodded, studying the tiny entrance beneath her. Her breath hitched in her throat. "Do you reckon so?"

"I really do," Su'la replied assuredly. "Because in my line of work, you see just how things can adapt and find harmony, despite what they come up against."

"How so?"

Su'la adjusted and sat cross-legged on the orange earth. "Well, take these little mice for example. There is no way a creature this small and weak would be able to survive out here in the heat and the wind, were it not for the skills it's developed. They don't just run around and eat what they can and pray there's shelter when the sun gets too hot. They have burrows... they have two entrances to stop them being buried... they use their wings to test the wind, to *make paths* over the dunes towards food and water. Now, some of that is instinct – great-parents, to parents, to children, and so on – but a lot of that is discovered. They *discover* how to adapt to life out here. They learn to survive, even in such small ways." She paused, then smirked. "Do you want to know something kind of interesting?"

My'ala nodded.

"Some of these mice have made a burrow near our village, just over the ridge to the south where the land is really flat. They venture into the settlement sometimes, taking a look around. They don't go into the houses much – although some have tried their luck – and thankfully our stockpile is secure enough that they can't get in and eat the food. But they also don't need to, because they've worked something out: when we deliver our dried foods to the store-houses, the carts we use can often drop some of it onto the floor. So, the mice have *learned* the rough point that the sun hits in the sky when we most frequently transport the food... and guess what? They're waiting by the houses already, to go and grab something to eat and take back to their burrow."

"That's amazing," My'ala exclaimed, imagining the tiny creatures scurrying about beneath her, scratching at their broad ears with little clawed feet. "I didn't realise they did that."

"We've observed it for a good few months now, since the last rains came through. But that means that, in the span of only *five years*, these little sand-mice have found a way to get food from us, without disturbing us at all."

My'ala considered the Headman's question again, floating around in her mind like a skater on the oasis.

"These little mice... they've learned to adapt to the desert, and live in harmony with it, and now with us too," Su'la added. "But it's not just them: it's what every animal and creature out here does to survive. We've seen it all around, this... sense of *being* that they have. There's this innate ability to *innovate*, and grow, and change. To live with nature, and never take more than it can give." She tilted her head to one side. "And does that give them great purpose? Probably not. I doubt the question crosses their little minds. But is it part of what they are? Of *course* it is... in the same way that we've proven it's part of who we are, out here in the oasis. Always surviving, always adapting...."

My'ala opened her mouth to speak, but no words came to her. Her breath stalled for a moment, her mind humming quietly. The flood of thoughts and fears that had been overwhelming her, stemmed their flow suddenly.

Opposite her, Su'la inspected the hollow pipe she had taken from her belt, and began assessing the ground between the two burrow entrances – seemingly unaware of what she had said, or how profound it had been. My'ala watched her work, almost in a daze, overcome with a sense of pride in her sibling.

So wise, and she doesn't even recognise it, My'ala thought, gathering herself and smiling softly. *Because she's right: we have adapted and grown to live out here in the Unknown. We have overcome so much and learnt from it along the way. We don't recognise who we are, compared to the people we were in Arbash, not because we've lost our way...*

...but because we've learned so much to get here.

"I may need a hand with this bit," Su'la acknowledged, looking up to My'ala. "Somewhere beneath us, between these two holes, is their egg chamber. We need to use this pipe to clear the earth above it without damaging it, then we can collect the eggs and cover it back over. Are you alright to do that?"

Distracted for a moment, My'ala took a long breath and nodded. "Yes... I am," she replied, shuffling slightly closer. "I can help." She opened her hands.

And then, I shall visit our resident Sand-King, and ask what he thinks about it...

VI

COMPLIANCE

Once the mouse eggs had been gathered – and Su'la had delicately covered the holes she had made with the hollow pipe – My'ala had excused herself from the expedition and raced off over the dunes to the north-east, off to where she had met the Sand-King the previous day. Her mind was alive with activity; as if uncorking a bottle, a deluge of thoughts came flooding out with no sign of stopping.

Moving with some speed across the Unknown, My'ala widened her stride and skimmed across the dune-crests effortlessly, navigating the peaks and troughs without an ounce of hesitation. Like Nehebu did; like the mice did, scurrying along the ridges with their folded wings. It gave her some confidence – both in her abilities, and in the wisdom she had received from Su'la – as she approached the rocky outcrop where the Sand-King had told her they would be waiting.

Once there, however, she stopped in her tracks. The confidence that had emboldened her lapsed suddenly. Because the basin beneath her, with the xenolith at the centre, was empty.

And of the Dragon Prophet, there was no sign whatsoever.

My'ala frowned and glanced about, wondering if she could be mistaken. Depressions marked the sand around the pit, evidencing where the great beast had lain recently. The shape of scales could be seen on the clay below, almost like imprints. But of the great beast and their smoking nostrils, My'ala could see no sign that they were there.

"Nehebu?" My'ala asked, puzzling at the basin of clay and rock. Then, calling louder: "*Nehebu!*"

Casting her ear over the sands, she waited for the hum and bellow of the Sand-King stirring from slumber. For the dunes to subside, and from within their walls a huge, scaly body to emerge. For a moment, the winds spiralled higher, and My'ala wondered if the Dragon Prophet had heeded her summons at last — only to find it was just the natural flow of the desert, coursing over the dune-crests.

Have they left for good? My'ala wondered, concern flooding her body. Artemis had not left her, even when the soldiers approached the gates of Arbash; Othella had not left her, even when they were close to starving out in the desert. Nehebu — a creature so vast and intelligent — had no reason to abandon them in their time of need.

Except that they admitted that they rarely involved themselves in human quarrels... that they often just passed them by. My'ala swallowed over a lump in her throat. *Perhaps the Sand-King has changed his mind... and deemed us a distraction that they don't need.*

Her doubts clouded her mind for several heartbeats: several

heartbeats that drummed in her ears like falling stones. My'ala breathed through it, bristling at a surge of wind that pulled up the side of the basin beneath her. It rippled through her robe; knots of her dark hair fell free of her cowl. She threaded them back behind her ears, glancing to the horizon as she did so—

Where she spied a torrent of sand lifting from the dunes, off the back of a huge creature – and My'ala sensed her relief return to her once more.

There they are...

They moved so quickly across the Unknown: the great Sand-King seemed to glide over the dune-tops, carving vast trenches through the sand. The plumes that arced through the air covered the blue for miles. The rustle of the parting sands crackled in her eardrums. Nehebu seemed to remake the desert before her very eyes, in the wake of their immense passage.

They did say one of their names was the 'Breach of the Dunes', My'ala recalled. *And from this, I can see why...*

Following their path over the Beyond, My'ala watched the Sand-King disappear behind the ridges ahead of her, the rumble of their massive body growing gradually louder as they altered course and made their approach. For a while, all My'ala could hear was the churning of the sand like ocean waves, filling her head until her own thoughts were lost.

And then, in a cloud of dust that coated the sun, the rumbling stopped, and a great head emerged high above her, looming over the rocky outcrop to observe her beneath horned brows.

"*You called?*" Nehebu the Dragon Prophet boomed, sparks flickering between their huge pale teeth.

"Did you... *hear* me?" My'ala asked, in a pique of amazement.

"I sensed your presence, but no, I heard nothing... it was your heart, little mouse, thundering like a storm that drew me here."

"Oh, I... sorry I was just..." She paused. "I wasn't sure if you would still be here or not, you see."

With that, a grunt of disbelief pulled up from the Sand-King's throat. *"An ancient such as I never forgoes a promise. Keep to your words, My'ala, and know I will always keep to mine."*

My'ala nodded. "Thank you, Nehebu."

"Take peace, little mouse. Now, to what do I owe these summons?"

"I believe I have an answer to the Headman's question," My'ala replied. "Or something very close, at least..."

An inquiring puff of smoke lifted from Nehebu's nostrils. *"Do you?"* they rumbled. *"How interesting... and you have faith in this answer?"*

"I... I think so. Yes."

"Hm... very interesting." The Sand-King bowed their head. *"If that is so... then please, go on. Elucidate for me, young one."*

My'ala stood taller and rolled her shoulders, weighing the words she wanted to say. "What we are... are innovators," she began. "We create, develop and grow. We nurture ideas, and advance both ourselves and the community around us. We are guided by our ability to change: to change ourselves and our outlooks. Our beliefs, and our ways of life. It all circles back to this almost animal-like need to do better, run faster, move further. It's something my sister sees every day when she researches the animals that live around the desert. Creatures that shouldn't be able to live out here at all... and yet survive and *thrive* anyway." She shrugged. "It feels like everything we do, we do to do better. To think wider and do more. I'm not sure if that makes any sense, but... that's the answer I came across. That's my sister's wisdom on the matter." *Even if she didn't realise it herself.*

Above her, the Sand-King shifted their snout and studied her. The wisdom of a thousand stars shimmered in their fiery eyes, as if the sun itself had fallen from the sky. *"An intriguing proposition, certainly,"* they admitted. *"I sense some merit in your conclusion, and the points you make. Very good."*

My'ala pursed her lips, sensing more to follow. "But...?"

"I will now ask you a question: not how *you prevail, and overcome these things... but more* why *you do so in the first place. You are creatures that adapt and grow, as you say... but* why *do you adapt? Why do you grow, and fill your minds with such possibilities? You are mortals, born of the sand and returned to the sand one day... what drives you to do more, and think in new ways, if that is the ultimate conclusion?"*

Listening intently, My'ala bit her tongue. She was reminded of the familiar sense of frustration that she had faced as a child in Arbash, and then as a traveller, moving across the Unknown. The feeling of being on the cusp; of reaching up for greatness like a fruit on a branch.

Only to have it snatched away at the last moment, by the wisdom of another...

"We are adapting our ability to survive," My'ala countered, rising to the challenge. "Or that's certainly who we are out here: a people learning to survive in more ways – and better ways – than before. Day by day, season by season."

"And perhaps an answer of survival would satisfy the tiny mind of a mouse, or a roving fox... but to mortals such as yourself, with minds that spread like the leaves of a palm, is that truly enough? Would your answer satisfy?"

"Perhaps. It's a simple answer that makes a point."

"*Do not mistake simplicity for conclusiveness, My'ala,*" Nehebu warned. "*I have charted these barren lands for generations gone... I do not believe I do such things simply to survive. And neither do you, little mouse. You are far more than that — and have so much more potential than that — even to an aged eye such as mine.*"

"But survival is surely at the core of who we are, regardless? If not for survival, then there's nothing to... be."

"*A cluster of reeds may survive many droughts before it perishes... are you to say that you are like reeds, swaying gently beneath the sun without ever being more?*"

"I... no, of course not..."

"*Because you don't just adapt to survive. When you do more, or do better, you are feeding a fire deeper within your soul, little mouse... are you not?*"

"I suppose," My'ala replied defeatedly.

Above her, the Sand-King drifted closer, the heat from the embers in their mouth pulling sweat from My'ala's cheeks. "*That is not to say I do not agree in part with your answer, however,*" Nehebu explained. "*One of the most intriguing things I have observed about your mortal kind is your ability to... overcome, shall we say, the adversities you face at every turn. And if that is what defines you, little mouse, then may you cry such truths from the highest peaks of this land. May you soar as eagles do, and fly to heights you could never imagine. It is a strength to overcome... and in you, I see such strength in abundance.*" They bowed their head sagaciously. "*I do not wish to dishearten you, My'ala. I only challenge the answer you have given with such... intensity, because it is missing something deeper. And because, if this Headman is as you describe, he shall find fault in any answer that involves growth and... change, as you see it.*"

My'ala frowned. "How so?"

"He has conquered lands and peoples. Cities have fallen beneath his armies. They pay homage to him as their ruler, through belief... and through fear. His is the word, and they shall follow it. So, any talk of change, or thinking larger than before... like a rotten fish, it will sit foul in his stomach. He is a man who has fostered blindness and submission in his subjects. He will not see adaptation as a good thing, but as a challenge..."

"Because if people are, by definition, always destined to grow in their minds," My'ala deduced, "then one day, they may outgrow *him* and his authority as well."

"Which is why, little mouse, such an answer will never satisfy the whim of this Headman. To concede your point and agree to it, would admit his own lack of control... which is something he appears incapable *of doing at every turn."* Nehebu snorted with disapproval, glancing for a moment across the sands to the west.

"That's completely true. He's proven that by coming here in the first place. He's only here, threatening us, because he cannot control us. He... he *will not* control us."

"And that defiance you must hold onto with both hands, My'ala," the Sand-King proclaimed. *"It is what separates you from mortals such as he. Do not lose that."*

"But that defiance can only get me so far," My'ala admitted. "His armies will come either way. The answer to his question is the only thing stopping that... and I'm still no closer to the answer."

"You are closer. Do not deny the steps you have already taken. Your sister's discovery, although flawed, has brought you to a new place: the how *has been realised, of who you are and what comes next. Now, My'ala, you must find the* why. *Find the core you are missing. Go to the roots, and find the source. Let its air breathe through you."*

My'ala swallowed; the sky seemed so bright above her. *I'll try,* she thought.

Taking a long breath – gritting her teeth – My'ala banished her doubt and nodded. "I will," she said, her defiance breaking through. "I will return to the village and think on it. I'll... I'll find something."

"I sense the spirits rally within you, little mouse. Channel them, and may they never abandon you." Above her, the Sand-King ran their tongue over their teeth. Slowly, they recoiled back over the sand ridge, the hairs on their chin fluttering in the wind. *"And I shall be here, for when you return. I will be expecting great things."*

My'ala looked into the fiery pits of their eyes again, then glanced back to their village in the south-west.

"I'll try," she whispered under her breath, the sky big and blue above her.

VII

STEWARDSHIP

The morning fell away to high-sun, and with it came the unbearable heat that the settlers of New Arbash had, over five long years, become accustomed to. The sun scorched the stones; vapour peeled from the banks around the oasis. The reed-beds beneath the palm trees wilted, hanging their heads like mourners. The very sand beneath their feet became like a furnace: if one ventured out without sandals, their heels would blister and scald. Even the fishers beneath their canopied huts sojourned away from the heat, leaving the fish to swim to deeper pools where the water was slightly cooler.

At high-sun, life in New Arbash seemed to stop altogether. The people took shelter, and awaited the dusk to bring cool air back to the sands. For many, it was a time to manage their homes, and cook meals for the following days. To catch up and rest, and take stock of the morning.

But for My'ala, who had paced about all morning with a sense of dread in her chest, there was no time for anything else to occupy space in her mind. So, instead of waiting out the sun, she had left her parents and Ki'lu at their family home and went out towards the northern-most tip of the settlement, to a place she often found herself going when she needed solace.

Or a moment of peace.

The village prayer-house was a thick sandstone building, with a narrow chapel that opened out on a domed cloister at the far end. Palm trees jutted from the open roof of the cloister, and thick bushels lined the wooden entranceway to the main hall. Red banners – bearing the God-Elect's crest – hung from the alcoves of the front pillars. Tall windows lined its outer walls, threaded with glass that imitated vines and flowers.

It had been one of Aurelius's projects, in the first few months after settling at the oasis. A personal endeavour, which he had at times taken priority with over even the more basic amenities. To argue his point, My'ala recalled how he had envisioned it being a sanctuary for the people: a place where, irrespective of their beliefs, anyone could go to give thanks or just gather among friends. That it would form a heart, almost, linking every aspect of their new home.

And, despite its lengthy construction, the God-Elect's vision for the prayer-house had manifested almost immediately: the walls had gone up, and people had gone to give offerings the very next day. Even as My'ala walked through its wooden doors then, she saw people gathered in the shade just inside, gifting small objects into little bowls on the walls.

I could take a pretty good guess at what their prayers will be about today, My'ala thought, relieved by the coolness of the air inside the chapel. Her skin prickled with the cessation of the heat, sending a shiver up her spine. *I know I'll be doing the same. We need as many of them as we can, with what little time we have left...*

Passing the palm-board benches and reed-woven tapestries lining the columns of the main hall, My'ala passed the plinth at the far end and stepped out into the dome of the cloister beyond. A narrow walkway formed its outer rim, lined with dried-reed archways, and the middle circle was a small garden fed from an underground spring. The life there was luscious and profound: spindly branching shrubs produced huge buds of gold and rose; thick grasses flushed up from the soil like threads of silk; columns of flowers pushed up like swords, alive with small insects and industrious bees. It reminded her of the hibiscus bushes in their home in Arbash, and the jade-leaved junipers lining the outer walls. Always teeming with life, no matter the season.

Full of a wealth and splendour that no coin could ever buy.

Stepping into the light again, My'ala embraced the cool breeze and the ripple of humidity from the cloister roof. It warmed her hands, and dappled her scalp with goose-bumps. The rustle of palm leaves issued from high above, eclipsing the ball of the sun beyond.

Looking down across the small garden, My'ala saw a figure knelt on one of the flat stones before the huge palm tree. Their robes pooled about them like a fountain, interlocking with the bends of the thick, green grasses. They held their hands in their lap, with their head stooped contently – lifting their gaze as My'ala approached to produce an effortless smile.

"Hello, my dear," Aurelius said, his pupils like seashells.

"Am I okay to join you?" My'ala asked quietly, charting the

path of a bee as it passed her head.

"You know you are. Of course. Please, come sit with me."

Acquiescing, My'ala knelt on the flat stone next to him and let loose a long breath.

The God-Elect reached over and clasped her hand, squeezing gently. "It's nice to see you, are you okay?"

"I think so." My'ala shrugged. "I went to speak to Nehebu again, out in the desert."

"Is that the Sand-King creature you spoke of before?"

"Yes, I... I spoke to him about an answer to the Headman's question. Su'la gave me an idea."

"What was her idea? And what did Nehebu make of it?"

"It was about who we were, and our ability to adapt out here in the desert," My'ala explained. "We are by nature innovators: we always want to change and improve. It's how we survive, it's... it's like a calling to us, from deep inside. This need to do more, and do *better*, at all things."

Aurelius nodded. "A very reasonable point."

"And the Sand-King agreed, or at least in part: they said it had merit, and that we *were* driven by that for sure... but it was missing something. It missed the 'core' reason, or... I wasn't sure what they meant."

"You found the *how,* but not the *why?*" Aurelius inferred.

"Yes, exactly that!" My'ala exclaimed. "Whatever that means, yes. That's what they said, and that's what I need to find."

"I can understand that. I see their point... but that's a lot to burden on one pair of shoulders. Especially with the time pressure you're under..."

"Perhaps, but I need to understand this. I need to know regardless." She looked to him, seeking understanding. "But I don't know where to start... I don't know what to look for."

The God-Elect met her gaze and nodded gently. He considered for a moment, as if scales were balancing in his head, but in the end he chose to remain silent. Instead, he squeezed her hand again, and let his eyes scale the height of the palm tree rising above them. The light washed over his pale skin, dappled with freckles and tiny wrinkles. He remained prostrated there for some moments, letting the wind ebb and flow in the cloister around them before he spoke again.

"Look up the tree, my sweet," came his soft voice. "Tell me what you see."

Look up the tree...? Puzzling, My'ala did as he said, looking up the tall trunk. "I see bark on the tree," she said. "I see insects. Leaves, high above. The sky and the sun. Lots of light, I guess."

Aurelius took a long breath. "And around you, what do you smell?"

"I smell..." My'ala inhaled. "I smell sweetness and flowers. Herbs and fragrances that remind me of ma's cooking. I smell fresh grass. Damp earth. Water... running over pebbles... chalkiness on the stones."

"And do you sense anything around you, as well? Any sounds that rise above the rest?"

"I hear the bees. Their tiny wings. I hear the chirp of small crickets. The waxy clicks of tiny beetles, hopping from flower to flower..."

My'ala rolled her shoulders; she sensed the knots pull free. The tremulations in her heart steadied, growing quieter.

Aurelius, still holding her hand, traced his thumb around her palm. "And what do you feel, now? What breathes through you, in this place, experiencing these things?"

"I feel warmth," My'ala admitted, with a blossoming deep in her soul. "I feel quiet. My head... it's like it's being held. Like *I'm* being held. And I feel so tired, I... I feel I could sleep forever." Her eyes closed and opened slowly; she yawned.

"It's rather magical, is it not?" The God-Elect rolled his shoulders. "Every time I come here, I feel just that way. That same sense of warmth and closeness. In this cloister, among these halls..."

Catching on to his meaning, My'ala raised an eyebrow at him. "So... are you telling me that this is...?"

"The God?" Aurelius said, a tiny smile of knowing creeping over his face. He looked from her back to the tree above. "A tiny fraction of Them... but yes, that is what I believe, at least. When we enter these places, and centre ourselves, that is where we are drawn: an opening, where They will come forth and bring us peace."

"But... how do you know?"

"I don't, because it's not about knowing... it's about *believing*. You see the signs, and interpret them." He smirked. "Do you think it's a coincidence that, when you felt that sense of warmth and quiet, the first conclusion you reached was the God? Why would your mind go there, if there was not some sense of truth in it?"

"Could it just be because I'm tired, and this space is very peaceful?"

"Then you could sit in a shady room anywhere, or out by any of the reeds in the oasis. You could put your hands together and lift your head, and think any number of things. But it would never feel quite right... it would never quite be the same as being in the God's house as you are now."

My'ala tilted her head. "I suppose."

"Because there's peace of the mind, which you can find anywhere... but there is also peace of the *soul*, which is something so much deeper."

"But what is the soul?" My'ala asked, sensing the warmth turn like a sleeping child in her chest. She could interpret the feeling as something close to a soul – something that was not physical, and yet seemed to be held in her chest – but exactly what that looked like had always alluded her.

"That's quite the question!" Aurelius laughed, drawing her thoughts back to the conversation. He closed his eyes for a moment, allowing the delicate warmth of the sun to wash over his skin. "The soul, in my eyes... is the unexplained parts of who we are. It is everything we have ever been, and everything we will ever become. It is memories, and dreams, and futures. It is faith, and hope, and the lines that connect every tiny coincidence we encounter. The soul is a vessel into which we pour ourselves, and from which we live and breathe. It is a gift, in my eyes, from the God above: the tiny part of Them that allows us connection to that higher place."

"So, when we see the light above, and feel that warmth inside as I've just done... that's us feeling the God in our souls?"

"For me, yes... that's how it's always been." Aurelius nodded. "Others may differ, but I have found solace in giving myself over to that belief: that my soul, my gift, is giving me the strength and the hope to continue. With its strength, I can do anything: it's who I am, unapologetically. So long as I act in goodness, my soul will always *provide* in goodness too."

It's who I am, My'ala recited, the words like wind-chimes in her ears. At the thought, the warmth in her chest eased over her shoulders, and the colours of the flowers ahead of her seemed to saturate and shine.

"Your soul is what guides you," My'ala interpreted. "What it represents, is what makes us who we are."

"We are, all of us, stewards in this land," the God-Elect proclaimed. "Both of ourselves, and the places we live. With the help of our soul – and of the God, too, for those who believe – we look after ourselves, and the places we eat. The places we gather, and worship, and build. Our bodies, and our minds. It is what provides for us, and helps us to overcome…"

To adapt and grow, even where it seems impossible to.

My'ala lifted her hand and placed it against the bark of the palm tree. The nodules and rivets of the wooden shell prickled against her palm. Around her fingertips, small beetles made slow progress over the bark; bees circled near her wrist, seeking the pollen in the flowers nearby.

With every breath, My'ala felt her heartbeat through her hand. Its delicate thuds rippled against the bark of the palm tree.

A soul to guide our path.

Bathed in warm light, with the delicate whistling of tiny birds in the alcoves overhead, she closed her eyes and whispered a prayer on the breeze.

And swore that she sensed someone listening: someone far, far above.

VIII

FALSE PROPHETS

"*You have returned,*" the Sand-King thundered, their nostrils like chimneys as My'ala gazed up at their wizened features. As promised, they had not departed from the rocky outcrop, and coiled tightly around its basin like a wicker basket. In the nadir of the afternoon sun, their scales shimmered almost like shields. "*And so soon, as well.*"

Catching her breath, My'ala peered up at the Dragon Prophet, using her hand as a visor against the light. Their size still sent a shock through her system whenever she visited: the sheer magnitude of such a being, who had traversed the Unknown for generations past. She had not believed such creatures existed: that they *could* exist, beyond the stories etched along the walls of Arbash's palace. Out in the wilds, nothing grew much larger than a fox; birds were no larger than sparrows. And yet, in the Beyond, there existed great beasts such as the Sand-King.

Makes me wonder how many there once were, My'ala thought, *and just how big they must have been, long ago...*

Above, Nehebu gazed off to the west – out towards the Headman's camp – with a dour expression. Their brow furrowed, interlocking the tiny horns jutting there. They had not looked at her since she had arrived: were it not for their comment about her return, she could have believed that she had not been seen at all.

Something is troubling them, My'ala deduced, nervousness plying at her chest. *Something has caught their eye, and they don't like it.*

But what could trouble something so vast and ancient? And what does that mean for us mortals?

My'ala thought of Ki'lu, and her family.

Are we safe?

"I have another answer!" she exclaimed, lifting her voice over her fears and the constant howl of the wind. "One that answers the *why,* as you said it should..."

My'ala ran her tongue over her teeth and waited. For a moment, the Sand-King did not respond. It seemed that they hadn't even heard her – that her voice had been lost on the breeze - which did little to alleviate the unease in My'ala's body.

But, after a few heartbeats, Nehebu tore their huge amber eyes from the horizon in the west and gazed down upon her, the ruminations of thought still sparking in their pupils – but what it was that they had been thinking, and what it meant, My'ala couldn't decipher.

"Another answer?" They grumbled under their breath. *"Are you sure, so soon? Remember my expectations are highest on this matter,*

little mouse."

"I assure you," she replied defiantly. "I believe you will understand this."

Nehebu cocked an eyebrow, impressed by her certainty. *"Do proceed then. I shall listen."*

"You asked me what guides us," My'ala began. "For the *why*, to how we adapt, grow and thrive as people. You asked for what drives us: for the essence of us that makes us... *us*. So I thought on it, and spoke to someone very close to me... and they gave me an answer." She swallowed. "The answer, is a soul."

A silence echoed out; the Sand-King studied her inquisitively. *"Implying...?"*

"What we are – and *who* we are – is determined by our souls: what came before, and what will come next, and what we choose to do in any moment. Our morals, and our beliefs, and our... our sense of self, and belonging. It is all contained in the same place – a place created by the God above, as some believe – but how we interact with that place, with that soul, is what makes us different as people. Unique, but also the same."

"I see... very interesting." The Dragon Prophet lowed their huge head. *"And this God that you say some believe in... do you? Are you a believer in the divinity, and the soul of the God?"*

My'ala paused. "I'm... I'm not sure. I think so. I believe we have a soul, and when I pray, I feel heard, but... it makes sense in some ways, but not in others. The person I spoke to, they have always believed, but I have never been completely certain..."

"Those who do not deny, believe," Nehebu rumbled. *"And wise are those who think in this way."*

"Wise?" My'ala puzzled, watching the Sand-King overhead.

"How so?"

"*Because those who do not deny, have nothing to lose... but those who deny, can expect their judgement when they return to the sands.*"

My'ala nodded, then paused. "Do... *you* believe in the divinity?"

Like thunder, the Sand-King shifted around the basin. A gurgle of sound escaped their toothy jaws, twitching the scales around their eyes and the hair on their chin – and it took several moments for My'ala to realise that it was laughter.

Are they... laughing at me? "What is it?"

"*Come now, little mouse,*" they boomed, their tongue flickering in their mouth. "*Look upon me. How could I, a being of such age, who conjures fires from their chest and reforges the very sands of the Unknown, not believe? I have existed for eons; I have seen entire peoples rise and fall. Are we to say that my existence is a mere* coincidence? *In the face of such truths?*" They bubbled with laughter again, shaking dust from the rocky outcrop in the basin. "*I am no coincidence. The eye, from which you gaze upon me, is made by no coincidence. The water welling from the oasis around your home, giving life in a place so inhospitable... that does not come by chance. It has all been divined, My'ala. It has all been guided by a hand. And you do well not to deny that, despite your hesitation.*"

My'ala nodded, her mind expanded out over the rolling dunes nearby. She had witnessed miracles, she knew – the very existence of Artemis and Othella had seemed to challenge all convention – and had always acted as if being guided by a greater force. The Prophets who had built Arbash, had built it from nothing but the stones at their feet. They, out in the desert, had then done likewise, with whatever they could scavenge.

Prevailing against the odds, she breathed. *Adapting and over-*

coming. With such truths, as Nehebu said, can we really say that it's only chance? That Arbash was made by luck, and we survive out here by that same luck? Can we deny something greater, guiding our souls, in the face of that?

"So, the soul and the God, is that... *the* answer?" My'ala asked, speaking tentatively like the first steps of a young child. "Is that the conclusion that we seek? Would it satisfy the Headman, despite his insecurity?"

At the mention of Nero's title, the Sand-King snarled with a flush of smoke. Their head twisted to face west again. In silence, the amber rounds of their eyes flickered and danced with disdain: almost as if they sensed the Headman, somewhere in the sprawl of the encampment on the horizon.

"*That it is* an *answer, we cannot deny,*" they said suddenly, their voice deep and assiduous. "*That it is a good answer — that draws upon the knowledge of our previous conversation — also cannot be denied.*" They paused, grunting. "*But even so, it is still not enough. Not to bring an end to your unease, nor to appease the whim of this Headman. He is a trickster... and into his trap, you threaten to fall.*"

My'ala sighed, her shoulders slumping beneath the folds of her robes. A pit opened in her chest, reaching down to the ground beneath her feet. Frustration threatened to eclipse her: knowing that the answer was still elsewhere, within reach but not yet in her hand.

And all because of that Headman's foul intentions, My'ala cursed. *Will he ever be satisfied with an answer?*

Or one that doesn't involve us falling beneath their swords...

"*I sense your disappointment, little mouse,*" Nehebu commented, their tongue twitching between their teeth. "*Do not be disheartened.*"

"But we still don't have an answer, and Nero will be

returning to the village with his soldiers *tomorrow*!" she cried. "How can I not be disheartened by this? That my people are in danger? We need something. *Anything*. What more could the Headman possibly want from an answer?"

Above, Nehebu exhaled with a trail of smoke and glanced down at her. Despite their supposed indifference to the quarrels of her kind, My'ala saw the glint of sympathy in the pits of their eyes. *"What more he could want, I do not know. Having watched his armies attack villages, and take control of towns, I wonder if anything could satiate a man such as he. All I do know is, a life guided by the will of a soul at the whim of the God will be anathema to him. He will not see the water, for the reeds that shroud it."*

"But why?" My'ala asked. "Why is that the case?"

As if levering the very sky, the Sand-King tilted their head. Thinking; considering. *"It is not a story to tell, as such,"* they said eventually, *"but is rather one to see for yourself."* They locked eyes with her for a moment, and My'ala sensed the enormity of the Dragon Prophet's mind in her head, pulling at the corners of her conscience. *"Do you carry with you a looking glass?"*

My'ala reached down to her side where, beneath her robes, the long column and glass lens of a looking glass lay holstered in her belt. "Yes, why?"

"There is something I wish to show you. I do not usually... accommodate, in such a manner... but I have been known to make exceptions."

"I... okay." My'ala swallowed. "What do I need to look at?"

"The truth." Dropping their head, the Sand-King placed their chin against the dune-crest next to her. Stood next to their eye, My'ala saw her reflection in its orb and shuddered. *"But first, you must acquire a vantage point. You must see as I do... feel as I do."*

My'ala blinked. Realisation crossed her face. "You want me

to...?"

"*Yes,*" Nehebu said plainly. "*Now do not keep me waiting.*"

My'ala blinked.

Okay...

Reluctantly, she stepped up to the side of the Sand-King's head, beneath the curved strut of bone that circled beneath their eye socket. Placing her hand against the scales, she felt the heat and the vibrations prickle over her palm and up into her arm. An unbelievable heat resonated from the beast's body, exuding from the embers that rattled in their throat. My'ala noted sweat on her brow, as she clung to the strut of bone.

And began to climb.

She moved slowly, more delicately than perhaps was necessary. Using the plates of the scales as hand-holds, she shuffled along the bony ridge. Clutching to the horns along the Sand-King's brow, she shifted up behind their eye. Sitting for a moment, she convalesced and nearly toppled at a gust of wind at her back.

Reaching the flat of Nehebu's scalp shortly after – between the huge coils of their horns – My'ala stood shakily. The cool air pulling over the dunes jostled with the heat of the sun, and the warmth that rose from all over the Sand-King's giant skull. My'ala felt each of their breaths as they vibrated up through her feet. From the vantage, she could see almost back to the village—

"*Hold on,*" Nehebu commanded—

And suddenly, she was rising higher.

Clutching to the nearest spiral of bone, My'ala swayed. Sickness ballooned in her chest. Adrenaline flooded her body, fear and excitement all merging into one.

The dune-crest slipped from view. The rocky outcrop

became a pebble, than a speck on the brown earth.

Still she climbed higher, as if touching the very sky itself – until Nehebu slowed, towering loftily above the desert, and tilted their head towards the horizon in the west.

"Now you see as I see," they thundered. *"Now you survey all that I have. The deserts I have forged for generations past…"*

Looking out on the world, the scale of it seemed impossible. In every direction, the sands rolled on without end. Rocks would occasionally jut from the ground; small hills would break the tedium of the dunes. In the hazy distance, she could make out mountains, little more than grey smudges where the land met the sky. But without those tiny breaks in the landscape, the world was completely formless. Plateaus after plateaus; dune-crests after dune-crests. For a few heartbeats, the view overwhelmed her. Dizziness swam in My'ala's head, and tightened around her lungs.

Until she looked out to the west – following the gaze of the Dragon Prophet beneath her – and saw the reason why they were there. The reason why she had ascended so high, to look out over the dunes. To a spot in the near-distance – a larger smudge – just beyond the basin of their village.

The camp, My'ala hissed, pulling the looking glass from her belt. *Where Nero's army await, sharpening their swords.*

"I see it," she exclaimed, lifting the lens to her eye. "It's just as vast as we feared."

"The Headman has amassed himself quite a force, over his years of occupation," Nehebu growled. *"I have seen many great powers rise and fall in this land… but few had larger armies than this."*

"How many are there?"

"A few thousand, I believe. The exact number is shrouded by their canopies."

My'ala gasped. *Thousands?* The population of Arbash had only been several hundreds. *Where could so many people have come from? How many places has Nero conquered?*

"We can't face this," she blurted.

Nehebu grumbled beneath her. *"Perhaps... perhaps not."*

"Is this what you wanted to show me?"

"Not quite." The Sand-King paused, studying the camp. *"Use your glass, and look to the fore of the camp, where the red flags billow atop the tents. Tell me what you see there, little mouse..."*

At their direction, My'ala passed her lens over the canopy tops, down towards the front of the camp where shade obscured the walkways. Eventually, she focused in on a larger tent with red flags around its entrance, where she saw—

"Nero," she gasped, feeling the same shudder of unease pass through her as it had done when she had first met him. The Headman skulked along the frontage of his tent in the same dark robes as before, his crop of ginger hair flushing around his oversized ears. "I see him there, at the front."

"My prediction was correct then," the Sand-King mused. *"There is indeed a fox among this den of mice..."*

"What's he doing? He's just talking to people."

"Observe, little mouse." Beneath her, she watched Nehebu's lips pull up in a sneer. *"Not at his words, but at his actions. Watch the fox flash his teeth, and snap at any who come close..."*

Holding her looking glass steady, My'ala did as the Sand-King said, and watched as the Headman circled and pulled at his robes with violent jigs of his hand. Nearby, she watched how soldiers quickly saluted or made their greetings; how the guards at the entrance faced forward with no emotion; how the servants, passing between, cowered away and nearly dropped to their knees. Nero walked about as if in a performance, cajoling anyone within reach. He barked commands and looked up to the sky and lamented the very sun. He wiped at the spittle around his mouth, kicking dust and threatening anyone who strayed too close.

My'ala watched, and sensed some justification at the unease she had felt. How, whether from afar or up-close, the Headman seemed to express only foulness. His every action was made with force; his mind seemed permanently fixed on it.

He rages, and they either respect or fear him, My'ala analysed. "What kind of man behaves like that?"

"One who has neglected sense for power," the Sand-King proclaimed. *"One who uses violence to proclaim."*

"But... why?"

"Because instead of seeking guidance from the soul, and from the God... he has chosen instead to imitate Them, and blur the minds of those around him."

At that, My'ala realised why the Sand-King had shown her the camp. "You've shown me this, and his actions... because how can I talk about a soul and a God as the answer to who we are, to someone who is so rotten to both?"

"And at that, you understand perfectly, My'ala. I am glad you see it too." Nehebu exhaled. *"Because souls are never rotten: it is you mortals that make them so. Ambition... power... greed... violence. A gift from the God is only a gift if you treat it as such. It does not require belief, although that undoubtedly assists in the matter: to be good, and act in mercy, are parts of the soul that any mortal can endeavour upon. But so many are blind to this, or ignore it. So many defy what the soul is destined for. In their own interests, they often forsake others."* The Sand-King growled at the horizon. *"And some... the worst of them... use that same power and belief to justify violence and hate. They imitate the whims of the God – the goodness and the peace – for*

their own cruel ends."

"By his own words, Nero has done that across the entire Unknown," My'ala said. "He's here, because he wants the power… he wants us to believe him to be a god too."

"Power is a weakness and a privilege. And for many, it's the difference in the flip of a coin. For too long, the Headman has chosen which side to look at… so much so, that he cannot remember that there is another side at all."

My'ala sighed, lowering her looking glass. The image of Nero's face leering towards her made her shiver and grimace. "We won't be able to negotiate an answer with him that makes him feel he is either smaller or weaker than someone else. Anything down that line will leave us vulnerable."

"Such is the fear of insecure souls."

"Which rules out hope, community, adaptation, the soul, the God…"

My'ala hissed between her teeth. *Everything.*

"None of those fully satisfy the answer of who you are, little mouse," Nehebu admitted, *"so they will sadly also not satisfy the cruel intentions of this Headman."*

"But there has to be something else," My'ala said, with determination. "Our ability to adapt and our closeness to the soul are two important parts, so there has to be a third thing that we're missing. Some other perspective I haven't found yet. And I *have* to find it: I won't just roll over and let them sweep through our village. I won't let people become slaves to Nero. That is no life to live, and I would honour my people better than that fate."

With a curl of the cheek, the Sand-King smiled beneath her. *"I have grown to admire your courage, My'ala. Perhaps you are not such a little mouse after all."*

"I just don't want to let the people down." She looked to her hands, rolling dust between her fingers. "I'm so afraid to fail them. They deserve so much better than that."

"*You are the hope that carried them out of Arbash,*" Nehebu exclaimed. "*You are the hope that carried them over the sands to your new home. This is your fight, and you face it with strength nonetheless. You will be the hope that gets them through this, as you have many times before… all you must do, is believe.*"

"I'll try, I will. I… I have to."

There's no other choice.

Glancing out into the distance, she passed her eyes over Nero's camp again. The sprawling canopies and billowing flags; the thousands of his army, with their swords and their shields. The scale of it all was massive, beyond anything she could imagine. The entire situation filled her with dread.

And yet we have to press on, she breathed, gritting her teeth. *Prevail, as we have done before. There is an answer somewhere out there. I just have to find it.*

Before it's too late.

IX

PURPOSE

Dusk fell over the blocky sandstone dwellings of New Arbash, bathing the village in a myriad of oranges and golds. They streaked the sky between thin lines of cloud, which ran east-to-west like the creases of a cloth sheet. The orange was immensely vibrant, not too dissimilar to the fresh clementines that had once grown across the valley outside Arbash: a memory that, although faded, still maintained its original lustre. But long shadows also fell over the settlement that evening: shadows that stretched across streets and rooftops, shrouding those who cowered behind their closed doors. There was none of the usual merriment that marked a traditional evening in New Arbash. No firepits were lit; instruments lay silent, hidden away so as not to draw attention. Like sand-mice sheltering in their burrows, the former citizens seemed to hide away and peer through the slats in their windows, looking out on the still waters and the beautiful sun marking the horizon in the west.

Reminded, at the same time, of what also lay in the west, just over the ridge that demarked the edge of their village. Of the fate that awaited them, at the hands of an army they could not match. The swords and gnashing teeth that would come with the rising sun, silhouetted on the horizon for all to see. Watching the world they had built for five years fall apart before their very eyes.

Watching everything that they had made, coming undone.

On her return from seeing Nehebu, My'ala had joined Aurelius, and had spent the evening preparing her people for the worst. It was not an eventuality that she had accepted, but she knew if she didn't keep busy, she would fall into a pit she could not crawl out of, filled with guilt and despair. So, with the God-Elect's help, she had busied herself with securing their stocks of smoked fish, eggs and vegetables; creating stockpiles in sandstone hollows to hide away people's belongings; showing children where to hide if they needed to when the soldiers came. She had even established an evacuation plan, in the event that Nero was somehow crueller than they feared. It was a sentiment that she was met with every time she encountered someone new in the village: *is there an escape plan if things get really bad, and who will lead us if the soldiers try and attack us?* At first, My'ala found herself at a loss as to how to answer; after a while, she began spinning a thread, which turned into a haphazard evacuation plan. But all of it skimmed over a larger truth that she found too painful to admit to them.

We are no safer in the desert than we would be under the boot of the Headman.

The thought made her sick. The idea of giving up everything

they had built together, felt like drowning. After the sixth recital of her evacuation plan to a young mother and her son, she had left their home to fall into Aurelius's arms, tears streaming down her face. The determination she had felt after her conversation with the Sand-King had begun to unravel.

We're running out of time, she thought softly. *We're running out of time, and have nowhere to go.*

"Maybe speak to your parents," Aurelius suggested, as they followed the long, meandering path back to their communal home on the dune-side.

My'ala – bathed in streaks of amber with her shadow stretched across the sand beneath her – took a long breath and wiped the last of the water from her eyelids. "You're right, maybe... maybe I should."

"I know you don't want to worry them, but sometimes our elders... they can see things that we can't. They're wise that way."

"Yea." My'ala scoffed. "You know, ma and I used to laugh about how my da was always right about everything when I was younger. No matter what it was, if he gave his opinion, it usually ended up coming true. He'd sit and work through something in his head, and give this big answer to the question, always full of insight. It was a skill of age, so he said... and we said he was just a wise old fool."

In reply, Aurelius smirked. "From my experience, he's at least two of those at any given time."

"Ha, well, you're right there." My'ala allowed herself to smile. "He always knew what to say... ma did, too, although she led more by the heart than the mind."

Aurelius nodded. "That's good balance. Both are needed for the best decisions in life."

"I think that's why they've stuck together for so long. They balance each other, without stepping on each other's feet."

"Keeping the peace, wherever they can."

"Exactly, I... I couldn't imagine them any other way."

"Neither me. It's been an honour to know them. They're both remarkable people."

"They really are," My'ala agreed.

And I love them so much.

Ahead – bathed in auburn hues – their family home rose from the dune-side like the shell of a tortoise, the windows like two beady eyes watching them approach. Along the rooftop, tiny birds flitted and darted between the small archways, their rose-brown plumage almost iridescent in the low light. They scattered momentarily as My'ala and the God-Elect reached the door, only settling again once the newcomers had passed inside and the stillness of the desert returned.

Within their home, My'ala stopped for a moment and let the *click* of the door latch echo through the chambers ahead of her. There were a few heartbeats of silence, before she heard a small gasp and the delicate padding of feet. Suddenly, movement issued from the dining room ahead of them: a flash of colour, moving down the length of the table.

And My'ala, watching the scene unfold, felt she could cry all over again.

"Ma!" Ki'lu screamed, her wild knots of hair bouncing on her shoulders as she charged towards My'ala.

Scooping her up in her arms, My'ala placed a kiss on her head and smiled at her. "Hello, my beautiful hummingbird!" she said. "How has your day been today?"

"I made sweet-cakes!" Ki'lu flashed her teeth, where the mixture lined her gums like syrup.

"Oh how lovely! Are they ready yet?"

"Not yet," My'ala's ma said from further away, stepping out from behind the cloth drape that separated the dining room from the kitchen. Her hands and clothes were chalky, covered in milled grain, and she had the prints of tiny hands over her arms where Ki'lu had clambered up to see the cooking pot. "They should be good soon though. The case is crisping very nicely."

"How exciting," My'ala replied, turning her attention back to Ki'lu. "And did you make them all by yourself?"

Her daughter nodded. "Yes I did."

With a glance, My'ala looked to her mother, who smirked and shook her head.

Beneath her, Ki'lu turned her head sheepishly. "Gr'ma *maybe* helped..."

"Is that so?" My'ala raised an eyebrow, before producing a warm smile. "Then I'm sure they'll be *extra* delicious."

My'ala gave Ki'lu another kiss, then put her down. Immediately, she grabbed My'ala's hand, a vice-grip around her wrist. "You have to see! Now! Come see!"

Hesitating, her heart leering, My'ala felt her daughter start to drag her into the dining room – before Aurelius stepped in, and replaced her hand with his own in Ki'lu's grip.

"I think your ma needs to speak to gr'ma first, my little star," the God-Elect said softly. Ki'lu seemed to despair for a moment, glancing between her parents. "But maybe you can show them to me first, and we can decide if ma will think they're as amazing as she says, yea? How does that sound?"

Like the flicker of a candle re-igniting, Ki'lu beamed and nodded, pulling Aurelius away towards the kitchen at the back of the room. He glanced back for a moment, smiling to My'ala;

she mouthed a grateful "*thank you*" as they disappeared behind the cloth drape.

Alone again, My'ala glided into the dining chamber and embraced her mother, who fussed about not getting any milled grain on My'ala's dress.

"It's good to see you, Mi-Mi," her mother said, holding her shoulders for a moment. "Your da will be through any moment now…"

As if on command, from the doorway off to their right, her father stepped over the threshold, his eyes brightening at the sight of My'ala opposite him. "Hello Mi," he said.

"Hi da," she replied.

"I wanted to say thank you for your help today with the stockpiles at the guard tower. I didn't get a chance to get there this morning."

"That's no problem. You know I'm always happy to help."

"Saved me a lot of work, that did." He stifled a shallow cough before nodding slowly.

"Aurelius said something about you wanting to speak with us?" her mother added, a look of concern crossing her bronzed skin. "Is everything alright? Or as alright as it can be, considering…"

"It's…" My'ala sighed. "It's actually that, that I wanted to talk to you about."

Her mother nodded, and glanced over to her father; he in turn gave My'ala an appreciative look, and gestured to the table between them. "Let's sit," he suggested, easing onto the wooden bench beneath him. "Just to save my legs, as much as anything…"

My'ala and her mother did likewise, getting comfortable on the palm-wood seats. My'ala felt tiny trembles in her hands and her legs, which eased when her mother closed her hands around her fingers. "What is it you wanted to discuss, Mi-Mi?" she asked, her eyes inquiring and full. "Is it about that question that that man asked you, the one who came yesterday?"

"It is… from the Headman of the camp over the ridge," My'ala admitted, a greyness cast over her face.

"What's happened?"

"I've tried to find answers to the question that they asked, but nothing fits. Or nothing that will satisfy *him,* at least, tyrant that he is. The worst thing is that we're running out of time, and I'm still no closer to it… and in the morning, Nero will be here with his soldiers, and…. and I…"

"Who have you spoken with about it?" her father asked.

"Su'la, and Aurelius obviously… a few people around the village as well, where I can. They all gave great answers, but… there were still parts missing. There's still *something* missing." She paused. "I mean, am I meant to know the answer to '*what are we*'? Am I meant to know that, at my age, with my experience of life? I've done a lot, I know… I've lived through a fair amount, but…"

Her mother stopped her, and squeezed her hand. "You don't have to have all the answers, Mi-Mi… most people don't," she explained, nodding.

"But *I* do… I do, because there's so much depending on it."

"I know it's a big task, and the timing is scary."

"More than scary: it's *terrifying.*" She shook her head. "How am I supposed to know my purpose and who I am, when all I can think about is what's on the horizon? How can I save all these people, when I can barely save myself?"

Her mother drew a long breath in and rolled her shoulders, sympathy crossing her gaze. There was knowledge there: a knowing, of facing similar predicaments. She met My'ala's gaze, tapping her hand twice, before her lips parted to speak again. "Tell you what, let me tell you a story for a moment. I don't know if it'll help with how you're feeling, but I know it'll make you smile. It's a story about me, from a long time ago... when I met a grumpy young man who swept me off of my feet, showing me who I was and who I could be."

"Um, okay..." My'ala smirked, and glanced across to her father; he winked at her, before gesturing for her mother to continue.

"We were courting for two years, having met one day out in the clementine fields of Arbash," her mother said. "I was out picking fruits, and your father was labouring over some machine I could never understand. He promised to show me how it worked, and other designs he had, if I dropped by his workshop later that day – which I did, and then did so every day for that entire season. Safe to say I found him rather pleasant company... even if the machines were a bit boring." Her father rolled his eyes; her mother smirked and continued. "Eventually we moved in together. I changed work and we settled. Things seemed really good. But as you're feeling now, there was something missing that we both felt but neither of us could quite work out. At first, we thought it was each other – leading to a few rather *tense* conversations – but then we realised no, it wasn't us. It was something else." A pleasant recollection illuminated in her mother's eyes. "So, one evening we sat together and prayed for an answer. We looked to each other and said that, no matter what, we'd find a solution. I didn't think much of it, and went about life as normal for a few tendays... until one day, when cooking a meal, I felt my stomach with my hand, and..." She smiled, her face opening like a book. "I couldn't believe it. I couldn't even grasp what it meant at the time. Your father was overjoyed: I remember him coming in that evening, sweeping me about the kitchen dancing. It just felt right... it felt like we had been answered. That that moment – feeling the life growing inside of me – was all I needed, to feel whole."

Her mother looked across to her da. Lifting his hand, he placed a hand against her cheek and brushed his thumb along her jaw.

"Happiest day of our lives, that was," her father explained. "And then the same again with Dur'al, and with you, Mi-Mi. Happiest days we've ever had."

"We didn't know what we had been missing," her mother added. "We didn't know how we would manage together, in that constant state of uncertainty. But then Su'la came along, and... it was just so obvious. It could have been nothing else."

"That's... beautiful," My'ala commented, looking between them both. Her heart felt light and warm in her chest; she recalled what Aurelius had said on the dune-side outside of the house.

They really are remarkable people.

"That's not to say children are the answer... not everyone shares that purpose, and that's okay," her mother continued. "But it's more what it represented: as soon as Su'la was born, we were no longer just two people. We were a *family*. We were part of something bigger than ourselves, and... I think that's what made it feel so special. That's what gave us that peace inside: knowing that that need – one that we didn't even realise *existed* – was fulfilled. We were part of something bigger, suddenly... and whether that's a child, a job, an idea or a journey, I think everyone has that feeling. Everyone has that need to fulfil."

"We all aspire to more," her father mused, "in this life together. Others find it in pursuing their passions; we found it in you little rascals. You were our gift to the world. Our best moments. Everyone has a gift to give... and if you haven't found yours, Mi, then that just means it's waiting for you out there, somewhere."

Aspiring for more, My'ala thought, feeling a sense of peace that she hadn't felt before. Like strings, the sentiment seemed to ripple between her parents, their vibrations finding harmony in the spaces between. *To be part of something bigger. A need to fulfil.*

A gift to the world.

"Although we have it lucky, you see, Mi," her father continued, lifting his hands joyfully. "Because now, we get to live our gift to the world all over again!"

My'ala – her mind alive with new thoughts – puzzled for a moment. "How do you mean?"

"Because you, Mi-Mi," her mother explained, squeezing My'ala's hand, "have given us more of a gift than we have any right to receive. A gift that the world should repay one hundred-fold. Your little Ki'lu... she is such a blessing to our lives, and after facing so much to get here and settle in this place..." Her face creased as she spoke. "It's different for everyone who experiences parenthood... but I can only imagine the amount of joy you must feel with her, as her mother. The amount of love that must feel your heart, seeing her. If it's anywhere near what I felt with you and your brother and sister... it's an amazing feeling."

For a moment, My'ala saw her daughter's face. She saw the freckled rounds of her cheeks, and the button-tip of her nose.

The thick knot of her hair pulled around her tiny ears. Her little teeth grinning wider than the widest dunes of the desert. My'ala thought of her stomping around, splashing in the oasis; charging off over the sands towards home; snoring softly in Aurelius' arms. The glint of intrigue and wonder in her eyes, as she looked out on a world she longed to understand, to grasp in the palms of her questing hands. The search for more; the constant need to know.

To fulfil something greater than herself, My'ala realised. *Because she, like us, wants to find her gift to the world.*

"She's my greatest joy," My'ala said aloud. "I love her so much, and would do anything for her. I... I cannot imagine a world without her. I'm so afraid of it, with..." Tears fell, but she held her cries back. "I don't know what will happen when they come. When Nero brings his army here. I don't know if she will stay with me, or if..."

Oh gods, please no.

Sensing her unease, her mother slid her hands over her back and embraced her, circling fingers against My'ala's back as she struggled to steady her breaths. Thoughts came and went; nightmares, many of them, flashed behind her eyelids. Of the Headman and his armies; their swords and shackles.

Ki'lu being taken away...

My'ala sucked air through her teeth and moved back from her mother, wiping her eyes with the back of her hand. "I would do anything for her," she repeated. "I would do anything..."

"I know you would, Mi-Mi," her mother replied. "And we would too."

"No matter what," her father added.

"But you're also *our* daughter, and if there's anything we can guarantee... it's that you'll find a way. You always have. In that, I don't think I have any greater trust in the whole of the Unknown. This may be bigger than anything you've faced before, but in the end it's only another hill to climb. And you're already climbing, Mi-Mi." Her mother smiled broadly. "You're already almost there."

My'ala nodded, her chest rising and falling. "Thank you," she said softly. "I... I don't know what I'd do without you."

"And we wouldn't know what to do without you, My'ala," her father admitted. "Always remember that."

Her mother bowed her head in agreement. "And whatever you need, we're there for you."

My'ala held a hand to her chest, over her heart. "Thank you, both of you... always."

"Of course." Her mother glanced over her shoulder, hearing sounds of giggling from the kitchen. "Is there anything you do need, before you go?"

My'ala shook her head. "No, I promise. But thank you. I'll take Ki'lu to bed soon, and then I think I'll go for a walk to clear my head. The night air usually does me good."

"That sounds like a good idea. Go careful out there."

"I will, don't worry."

I promise.

Lifting to a stand, My'ala stepped away from the palm-wood table and blew a kiss to her parents, squeezing her ma's shoulder as she passed.

Turning to the cloth drape that sheltered the kitchen space behind, My'ala cleared her eyes and steadied her heartbeat, shaking off her hands as she did so – already smiling, as the quiet whispers of Aurelius and their daughter drifted over to her, giggling about sweet-cakes and tiny hummingbirds.

X

FATE

With the moon arcing overhead, and the last remnants of the sun's light cloaking the horizon in the west, My'ala climbed the ridge to the south of their village and started walking. She had no destination in mind, and carried nothing but the robes on her back: but regardless, she pressed on into the emptiness ahead, hoping the cool air and the porcelain glow of the moon could help ease her tired mind.

The dunes were flatter and longer in the south, like wrinkles on the bark of a tree. There were no rocky outcrops or plinths of stone jutting from the sands. Nothing to demarcate the world and its landscape. In the day, one could see so far ahead that the sky seemed to swallow the desert.

At night, however, that same nothingness felt smaller and more intimate. Like a painting, My'ala's presence was a focal point against a backdrop of black and blue. She floated ghost-like over the dunes, with only the whispers of the wind to keep her company. Other than that, the Unknown was exactly as it was named: an expanse of space, silent and still, that ancient cartographers had overlooked on their maps as nothing but sand and sky. The city of Arbash had been the sole landmark, along a coast of high cliffs and azure-blue seas. Everything beyond that – in every direction as far as one could travel – had been beyond comprehension. Many cartographers had left it blank in their sketches; others had scrawled beasts of legend on the thin parchment, gifting wonder to a place so destitute of it. As a child, My'ala had thought the two images – the beasts and the barrenness – had been some sort of strange contradictions.

But after Nehebu, I see that they're actually one and the same, My'ala considered, gazing up at the first stars glinting in the sky above. *This land is a place of disbelief. A nothing that holds so much mystery. The Sand-King is but one example, and perhaps New Arbash is another. A place that defies belief.*

A home, to many who once denied.

Looking behind, the bowl of the village was a small dip in the horizon, as if the God had reached down and pressed their thumb into the desert. The dull red of dusk created a strange mirage across its ridges, streaking down its sides. Without knowing its location, she would have hardly recognised there was a village there at all: only the faint glow of torches discerned the settlement that lay within. A settlement that was slowly drifting to sleep.

Awaiting what comes tomorrow.

A cold wind whipped up behind her; My'ala pulled her robes tight across her back, shivering. The ground beneath her seemed to shift beneath her weight, pulling away from her sandals. It was almost as if the thought had conjured the wrath of the desert, uprooting nature all around her. For a moment, she was terrified: more terrified, even, than she had been when faced with the prospect of Nero.

Until, like a rush of seawater over pebbles, she heard the crackle and shift of the dunes on her left, reverberating up through her legs as if the entire Unknown was going to swallow her up—

And, from beyond the nearest ridge, a scaly head emerged, their mouth aglow with the orange of embers.

"Little mouse," Nehebu grumbled, their tongue flashing with sparks. *"I wondered where I might find you."*

"How did you know I was here?" My'ala asked, confused.

"Your steps may be light, but your heart thunders like a storm." Snaking around the dune-side, the Sand-King lifted their head, their massive skull and barb-like horns glowing softly in the moonlight. *"I sensed trouble... and so I have come."*

Despite the coldness of the desert at night, the heat radiating from the Sand-King's jaws was enough to make My'ala wipe her brow. "I see, I..." She paused in thought. "Why is your mouth so fiery?"

"Because I am old, little mouse... and this body of mine does not work as it once used to."

"How do you mean?"

They opened their jaws, letting a cloud of smoke filter into the night sky. Between their huge teeth, My'ala could see the maw of flame deep within their throat: as fiery as their amber eyes, aglow like the sun. *"The frigidity of the night air cools my body: my scales, and also the workings within. It is a pleasant sensation, after so long in the heat, but it is also dangerous... for if the embers in my chest grow too cold, I become weak and ill."* They lifted their head momentarily, exposing their neck. Down their throat, threads of yellow expanded between the scales, as heat exchanged up from their chest to their mouth. "*So, I must stoke these embers, and exhume the flames to keep my body warm. It is a tiring process, but necessary to combat the chills of the night.*"

"You have to release flames to warm your body, so it doesn't become too cold?"

"*Yes, precisely so.*"

My'ala nodded, her curiosity piqued. "Can I... can I *see* the fire? Can I see you breathing it? I... I just thought I would ask. I can't imagine I'll have the chance again..."

With a turn of their grey-haired cheeks, Nehebu grinned down at her. "*You know, little mouse... I was hoping you'd ask that.*"

Turning their head to the rolling dunes behind them, the Dragon Prophet made a low, guttural sound that prickled the hairs on My'ala's neck. She watched the embers burn brightly, suffusing with energy until their entire mouth seemed to be awash with yellow and gold.

Then, with a click of their tongue, the Sand-King exhaled – releasing a jet of flame that burst over the sands.

My'ala gasped, entranced by the fire as it jetted over the dune and curled up at the edges. Molten colours fuzzed in her vision: reds and ambers and yellows and whites, in shades she had never witnessed before. Like a spout, they poured from Nehebu's lips, rippling between the curved fangs in their jaw. It seemed to last forever, alighting the desert like a fallen sun – until, with a tiny breath, the fires were extinguished, and all that remained was a smoking trail from the Sand-King's mouth.

"That was... *unbelievable*," My'ala exclaimed, following the Sand-King's head as they turned back to her. Across the dune bed where the fire had burnt, My'ala noticed tiny, twinkling dots scattered over the sands.

"*It is quite a spectacle to the unfamiliar eye,*" Nehebu replied, the fiery glow softening in their throat.

"And that twinkling there, in the dip of the dune... that's glass, isn't it?"

"*Very observant of you.*"

"Does that always happen, when you... breathe the fire?"

"*The fires from my embers contain a heat that the sands cannot withstand... so in their place, this glass is made, to mirror the stars high above.*"

"I don't think I've ever seen so much glass in one place." My'ala lowered to a squat, studying the tiny shards. "It's nearly impossible for us to make out here, without the tools we had in Arbash."

"*Then please, gather as much of it as you can, little mouse. Perhaps this may be a beginning for you, so you have the tools to make more.*"

My'ala winced, thinking of the future – *of so much uncertainty*. "Thank you for showing me this," she said nonetheless. "I... as I said, it may be the only chance I'll ever get to see it, depending on what happens tomorrow..."

Opposite, Nehebu lowed their head to her, their expression measured beneath the curl of their horns. "*Do not worry about tomorrow, little mouse,*" they advised. "*Tomorrow can worry for itself.*"

"Can I ask you something, Nehebu?" she asked suddenly, lifting to a stand again.

"*You may.*"

"Do you ever aspire to do something greater than yourself? Do you find joy in... in giving something back to the desert, or to those who inhabit it?" She paused. "I don't know if it's the same for someone such as you, but... I thought I would ask. Just to see."

"*Something greater than myself, you say?*" The Dragon Prophet exhaled a puff of smoke, thinking. "*Well, I have traversed these sands for so many generations gone — watching kingdoms fall, and peoples rise, buried by the constant churn of the Beyond — that I fear I often lose that sense of perception. I believed... and have always believed... that my destiny is to grace these sands forever, reforging the desert again and again as a farmer tills their soil. To facilitate a role; to become part of the Unknown itself.*" They paused. "*So, yes... perhaps there is some purpose in achieving that which is greater than I. For I do not reforge these lands without an intent, after all... even if that intent has long since been lost to me, or may never be realised until I am long departed.*"

"And do you fear that?" My'ala asked.

"*Fear what, little mouse?*"

"The not knowing. The idea that you may die, even after so long, having never found why you lived in the first place. Does that not scare you?"

"*No,*" they replied plainly, without hesitation. "*No, I do not fear it... because that is a part of my journey. That is part of my place, as a Prophet in this land.*"

"But... how?"

"*My legacy, little mouse. My gift, to those which come after me.*"

My'ala's ears pricked. "What do you mean by '*gift*'?"

"*I have built this desert with my own body, for reasons I may never know... but sometimes, I see the fruits of my labour in those that it impacts.*" They glanced over her head, back towards New Arbash. "*One day, I would have slept in the basin where your village lies, digging away at the dunes just enough to form an oasis. Not for any purpose that I was aware of, or with any intention in particular...*

but then, one day, I found you tiny mortals there, building a new life in that small place, and it all aligns. It makes sense. With or without intention, there is always a larger work at play. One that I am as much a part of as you are."

My'ala nodded, her mind spinning like the gears in one of her father's old machines. "So... there is always a greater purpose? There's always the desire to give back to the world?"

"For some, yes."

My'ala blinked. "For *some*...?"

"Yes: and that is where the fallacy of your people comes into play." The Dragon Prophet licked their teeth. *"That is why I often find your kind detestable to be around, or engage with."*

"How so, though? What *fallacy?*" My'ala inquired. "I don't understand..."

"Giving back to the world... seeking a greater purpose... for many, it is not a desire: it is a choice that they choose not to take," Nehebu explained, a bitterness, centuries-old, rising in their chest. *"For many, taking is greater than giving. The greatest purpose is not to serve others, but serve themselves. What they acquire, is only ever theirs; what they decide, is only ever done in their interest. Selfishness has plagued your kind for generations past; countless leaders have climbed over their kin to achieve their aims. Power, greed, deceit, subjugation: it all serves no ends. It is all purposeless, beyond the whims of one. The undeserving rise ruthlessly, while the deserving are crushed under the weight of their own good intentions. It has swallowed entire kingdoms, and crushed people to dust. I have seen it all. I have watched it, and turned away in despair. No-one learns, and the leaders still clutch at power for themselves..."*

"Like Nero has," My'ala rasped, shaking her head.

"Precisely so, little mouse."

"Nero doesn't serve his people, he only serves himself.

Anything that keeps him in power. Anything that maintains control. So the idea of a greater purpose as an answer to who we are is futile, because…"

"*The only greater purpose that the Headman seeks… is himself.*"

My'ala placed her head in her hands and rubbed at her skin, prickling the fine hairs over her forehead and cheeks. The wrinkles beneath her fingertips were like trenches; her skin was dry and coarse like sawdust. She had no tears left to offer for her frustration, so only found the strength to sigh and look to the stars, glittering absently far overhead.

"What are we supposed to do?" she asked the night sky. "How are we meant to find an answer?"

"*I am not sure, My'ala,*" Nehebu replied on the sky's behalf. "*This Headman is pernicious: he has only presented this question to you, in anticipation that you will never be able to answer it.*"

"Then it's not possible… we have no way to survive this."

The Sand-King remained silent, their huge amber eyes expressionless and still.

"Can *you* do something?" My'ala looked up to them, a tiny glow of light sparking in her heart. "Can you help us? You've seen his cruelty before. You know how he works, and our chances of success. I know you don't interfere in our lives… and want nothing of our kind or our ways… but, just for us, could you not just go to the camp and start—"

"*No,*" Nehebu growled, a sharpness to their voice. "*I will not.*"

"But… why?"

"*Because I do not meddle in your affairs, like you have said. I do not become like your kind.*"

"How would you become like us… or *them*?"

"*Because If I were to intervene, and make a ruin of their camp, sending them scattering into the Beyond… then how am I any better than this Headman? How is my wrath any better than that which he will inflict on you?"*

"Because you're *protecting* us from danger… you're fighting against a cruel man—"

"But it is not just him. It is his people, too: innocents who have lost their way. If I were to act, I would be forcing his people away, to face an unknown fate, just to protect you and those loyal to me. In doing so, I would be serving my own interests. Protecting my own. How is that any better? How is my cause, in its intention, any more deserving than his?"

"Because you won't be serving yourself, you'll be helping *us*," My'ala pleaded. "You won't subjugate us, or make us your slaves. We need you, and you have the power to do something about it… so please, *help!*"

The Sand-King closed their huge eyes, the embers in their throat becoming cold and still. A thousand tiny reflections shimmered across their scales, from the glowing orb of the moon high above. *"No… I will not play a part in your conflicts,"* they thundered definitively. *"I will not twist a fate that is not my own. I have entertained this, insofar as advising you, but I will stray no further into this matter. Fate is fate, and is no place for Prophets. If your plan is to use me to fight for you, then you shall come away from this with only disappointment. I am sorry, My'ala. I have decided."*

As their jaws fell closed, the light that had flickered to life snuffed out in My'ala's mind. Having prepared a response, she blinked and closed her mouth instead, sealing her lips like an ancient tomb. Accepting fate: a reality she could hardly countenance. Above her, the huge Dragon Prophet watched her resignedly, tiny flashes of hesitation peeling from the flames in their throat.

They won't help us, she thought, more as a shocked realisation than a matter of fact. *They have lost faith in our kind. They despise tyranny so much, that they won't intervene. They'd sooner let us fall beneath the sword of Nero, than to be accused of being like him.*

Because...

"Nehebu."

"Yes, little mouse?"

"You told me a story earlier, about a town on a river," My'ala recounted. "How Nero came with his army, as he does with us now, and he gave them three days to answer his question. And the people of the town fell apart and started fighting, with many of them fleeing across the river..." She paused, meeting their huge eyes. "You tried to help them, didn't you? You intervened on their behalf. You tried to help them cross the river, promising them it would be safe... and then..."

Above her, Nehebu glanced momentarily to the distant village, donning an expression that could almost be described as shame.

My'ala inhaled gently, sensing their unease. "I'm right, aren't I?"

"The Headman had surrounded his camp with metal spikes... there was no way through, even for one as large as I," the Sand-King recounted, full of sorrow. *"No matter how hard I tried, I could not reach his camp or his soldiers. I could not expose myself, for fear of being discovered and hunted. But even so... I wanted to help those people trapped in the town. I wanted to do something for them, if I could. So, to those who had survived the infighting, I made myself known, and suggested a path across the river that would save many of them. I used my body to block the worst of the fast-flowing waters, and led them to their rafts to travel across the river while the soldiers of the*

Headman advanced..." They paused. "*But the rafts... they did not hold. Many came apart. They were swallowed by the water, and swept downstream. I saw their bodies disappear beneath the white-wash; I went to help, but I could not save them... because my body was blocking the worst of the rapids, protecting those survivors who had found a good current. So instead of helping, I had to lie there, protecting the few whose rafts had held... as the others who I had promised to help, drowned before my very eyes...*" They flashed their teeth, the fire brightening in their chest for a moment.

My'ala took a breath, bearing the weight of the story. "And since then, you've kept clear of us... because the same thing may happen again?"

"*I am The Breach in the Dunes. The Storm-Soother. The Dragon Prophet of Old. I have reforged this desert for generations past, and will continue to do so until I depart this land for good.*" Nehebu circled back from her, twisting against the dune-side. "*But interfering in the conflicts of your kind... that is something I will not do again. Not after what happened. Not after what I did.*" They paused. *"I am sorry, My'ala, for what you must face. I am sorry that the odds are not in your favour. I am sorry that, despite my power, I will not come to the aid of your people in this time, against the Headman and his armies.*"

For a moment, they hesitated, and My'ala witnessed the conflict raging in the vast expanse of their mind – a tiny crack in the door, which was immediately slammed closed with a hiss and a snort of smoke.

"*I pray your spirit holds tomorrow,*" they rasped. *"I pray your soul is strong, and you stay the course you choose. May you be the light and the hope that guides your people to safety that day.*"

Without another word, the huge Sand-King drifted back into the shadows where the moon couldn't reach. After a few heartbeats, they were lost from sight, eclipsed by the Unknown ahead.

Stood on the dune-side, My'ala swayed gently as if about to collapse. A weight set against her shoulders, impossible to carry and impossible to unload. She blinked into the open air where the Dragon Prophet had been, to find only emptiness and cold air remained.

They will not help, she mumbled within. *We are alone.*

Turning, she saw the soft glow of fires over the furthest ridge in the distance. In a basin, where her people lay sleeping, their dreams plagued by nightmares of the following day. The people who, five years ago, had built a home from nothing. A people who, by high-sun, would lose it all for nothing. The last remnants of Arbash, living out under the stars.

With no prayers left, My'ala pulled her cloak about her body, and began the long walk home.

XI

MEMORIES

They had built Ki'lu's crib when she was only a few months old, having kept her in a cushioned basket with them when she was born. The crib was based by a slab of stone, into which had been scored several deep lines that housed the slats of the main bed. Like a longboat's hull, curved pieces of palm-wood splayed open from the middle, cupping the padded pillows inside that were filled with feathers and dried reeds. A dyed blanket lay over the top of them, made of a soft woven fabric, with other pillows and a thin sheet for Ki'lu to sleep beneath. Dangling overhead, the tiny shapes of metal hummingbirds spun on thin bits of thread, which danced with the colours of the candle that flickered in the corner of the room.

For the first few months, Ki'lu had cried often, being left in a bed by herself. Sometimes, she cried so loudly that they had been forced to put her back in the cushioned basket, even though she was growing fast and the basket was far too small. Eventually, they allowed her to stay in bed with them, carrying her off to her own crib when she was in a deeper sleep. They had cherished those moments, without admitting it to their daughter, knowing soon things would change.

And, after a few more months, they did change: like a tiny fox cub, Ki'lu slept peacefully through the night, often nestling so deep in her crib that she was half-sunk by sunrise. Sensing she had adjusted, they repurposed the basket to carry rations from the storehouses, and the pillows they used to cushion the benches along the dining room table.

Returning to Ki'lu's room then, My'ala stepped up to her daughter's crib and looked down on her sleeping body. The room was cool and quiet, the hummingbirds circling gently overhead. Ki'lu, tucked in on herself like a flower bud, embraced one of her pillows, kicking softly against the sheet as if running from something in her dreams.

My'ala reached down and pulled the hair away from her face, studying her features. Her soft eyes and her soft cheeks and the tiny line of her lips. The fragile nature of her, tucked up in a ball. Away in dreams as bright as stars.

My little gojan fruit.

My'ala remembered her first steps. Her first laugh, and her first smile. The smell of her hair after she had been sleeping. Her grabbing hands, plying at My'ala's arms as she spoke.

She had been a miracle. A blessing to her and Aurelius. The stars had shone in her eyes, with so much intrigue that My'ala could hardly fathom them. She was strong and pure; she was defiant and mischievous.

The brightest light in the sky.

In that moment, the fate of the next day was far away. The army decamped on the horizon was a sour thought, plucked out like a cactus thorn. In that moment, it was only her and Ki'lu. A mother, and her daughter. Time was distant, and irrelevant.

There's only here and now.

Shifting onto the bed, My'ala led down and nestled in next to Ki'lu on the pillows. Tucked against her belly – as she had been when she was growing – her daughter mouthed a few small noises before settling again.

My'ala lay her head on the pillow, and looked down at the crown of Ki'lu's head. She stroked the thick hairs there softly, threading them between her fingers. Almost instinctively, her daughter nestled against her chest, sensing the warmth and familiarity of her mother nearby. Their heartbeats seemed to match as they drew close. My'ala wrapped an arm around her, which she pawed at with her tiny hands.

My'ala breathed and shuddered. A quiet sob eased from her lips. *My little gojan fruit... my little star,* she whispered, feeling the droplets of tears in her eyes. *Thank you for everything... thank you for your life. You are my treasure. You are a gift to the world.*

Keeping very still, My'ala closed her eyes and listened to the rasps of Ki'lu's breaths, before she too was carried off into a shallow, restless sleep.

The candle flickered softly. The hummingbirds spun overhead.

And beyond the house, the night sky glistened, awaiting the coming dawn.

XII

KINSHIP

She awoke the following morning, stirring with gentle stretches of her limbs, to sense immediately that something was wrong – or rather, something was different. My'ala pulled the hair out of her face, and rested her hand against the feather pillows beneath her. The room was still, the candle in the corner having burned down to its wick. Light filtered down through high windows along the alcoves of the room, coating the crib in a warm, orange glow. Tentatively, My'ala placed her hand down at her side, hoping to hold her daughter close.

But instead, all she found was empty space, the pillows still warm with the recent presence of another.

Where's Ki'lu? My'ala thought, her mind struggling to catch up.

Slowly, her other senses began to adjust, revealing more of

the world around her. She lifted her head, wincing at the headache that stirred in her skull. Sounds returned to her first, which she deciphered with a narrowing of the eyes: the echo of whispers and quiet words nearby, accompanied by the rattle of pans. The noises filtered through the cloth drape across from her, separating Ki'lu's room from the wider house. Glancing over, she saw shadows shifting there, going about small tasks in near-silence so that she wouldn't notice.

Lifting from the crib, My'ala placed her feet down on the cold stones and noticed her sandals had been moved, and on the small drawer nearby a fresh robe had been left for her too. Puzzling, she reached over and unravelled the thin cloth, before numbly getting dressed and slipping the sandals onto her feet. As she did so, she also became aware of numerous smells filtering into the room along with the noise: the aroma of herbs and rich aromatics, and the infusions of fresh leaf teas. They were very homely smells, reminding her of her mother's cooking; My'ala relaxed her shoulders almost immediately. Adjusting the bindings on her shoes, she stood properly and inhaled again, summoning saliva on her tongue and grumbles of hunger in her stomach.

What is happening? she thought, wiping the tiredness from her eyes. *The day is almost full... why has no-one gone out?* Stepping forward, she stood before the cloth veil leading into the other room. *Suppose I better see what's going on...*

Clutching at the fabric, she drew it to one side—

Where, from the left, Aurelius appeared suddenly.

"Ah!" he grinned, sweeping an arm out. "Good morning! You're just in time..."

"In time for... *what*...?" My'ala queried, as she looked out on the dining room ahead of her—

And pressed a hand over her heart, joy and disbelief filling her soul.

Her family had gathered together, sitting around their palm-wood table amidst an incredible display of food. There were soft fruits and sweet meats and skewered lizards; a bowl of broth full of vegetables and decadent oils; flatbreads and small loaves on tiny wicker platters; sugar-crusted nuts and seeds topped with miniature flowers. Utensils had been laid out with serving spoons and knives. Ornate cloth squares, laced with red and gold, dotted the outer edge of the tabletop. Candles had been lit, swelling the room with light and warmth and splendour. My'ala looked across it all, her mouth motioning but with no words emerging.

"What's all this...?" she said eventually, being guided by Aurelius to the nearest seat.

Opposite her, her mother clasped hands with her father, who in turn clasped hands with Su'la. Meanwhile, racing around the end of the table, Ki'lu rushed up to My'ala and clambered onto the wooden bench, occupying a space on her lap with a churlish smile.

"I... don't understand," My'ala repeated, still unsure. She ran a hand through Ki'lu's hair, who swung her legs wildly and tapped her hands on the tabletop. "Why have you done all of this...?"

"Because... we don't know what today will bring," her father replied, meeting her gaze. "We don't know how it will end, or what will happen to us all afterwards. We know there's a risk... we know the consequences of that. It's something we cannot control." He paused. "But one thing we can control... is what is right here, right now. That is in our power. What happens later, need not affect us here – let our future selves make light of that." He raised his cup, joined by her mother and Su'la. "So for you, Mi, our prophet's star, the one who has led us so far and kept this family together... we wanted you to have one last moment doing what you love most. To dedicate time being here, as one family, all together. Because we may not know what today will bring... but I know I won't let my beautiful daughter face it on an empty stomach."

Tapping his cup with the others, he lifted it across the table towards My'ala.

And My'ala, with her soul close to bursting, lifted her own cup and tapped it with her father's.

"Thank you... thank you all of you, for this," she said gently, placing a kiss on Ki'lu's head and squeezing Aurelius's hand next to her. "You really did *not* have to..."

"There's a have, and a *want,* Mi." Her father bowed his head. "And believe me, we all wanted to do this for you."

My'ala nodded, as if a thousand blessings had suddenly been poured over her head. "There aren't words to say how much this means to me. I don't... I can't even explain it." Her smile became soft and introspective. "I suppose all I can say is that, whatever happens today, you are the most incredible people in my life. You are all a gift, and I will stop at nothing to keep you all safe and free together."

"We wouldn't change it for anything, Mi-Mi," her mother replied, the tiny shimmer of a tear in her eye.

"You do us proud, and we want to honour you where we can," her father added.

On My'ala's lap, Ki'lu wriggled forward and clamped her arms down on the table. "Now let's *eat!*" she exclaimed suddenly, reaching for the nearest spoon.

My'ala laughed, her face full of joy, followed by Aurelius

and her parents.

"Her highness has spoken!" Su'la chuckled, reaching for her own utensils and passing a bowl across to Ki'lu.

I am so blessed to have you all, My'ala thought. *Blessed in ways I can never describe.*

With a full heart, under warm candlelight, she helped her daughter take her first spoonful from the bowl – surrounded by wonderful smells, and a joy only found in family.

They had eaten well and drunk merrily before the knock at the door came. It reverberated through the house, like the drums of some ancient spirit. Their conversations drew silent, as their eyes turned to the door; her father, rolling his tongue over his teeth, beckoned the newcomer to enter.

The door opened, and from the bright space outside one of the God-Elect's guards appeared. They stepped into the dining room quietly, as a gust of air disturbed the light of the candles.

"I'm sorry to disturb you, your Highness," they said, directing their attention at Aurelius. "Our scouts have seen a small force approaching from the enemy camp. We believe the Headman is among them. They… they're armed, too."

Aurelius swallowed, and turned to My'ala. Meeting his soft eyes, she nodded and rose from the wooden bench.

"Stay here, and keep each other safe," she said stoically, fighting an unease that seemed to swell and grow in her heart. "Whatever happens, do not leave this house until it's safe to do so. I should be back soon, but if I'm not…" She paused; her hands shook. "Protect yourselves… and be strong."

Looking down, she saw Ki'lu peering up at her, her eyes big

and scared. Offering a fearless smile, My'ala leaned down and placed a kiss on her forehead.

"Be safe, little hummingbird," My'ala said, stroking her hair. "I'll see you soon. I promise."

Turning from the table, she nodded to the guard, and followed them out to the front door.

With trembling hands, she steadied her breath.

Time to face our fate.

XIII

THE BRIDGE

From the west, they approached under the haze of the mid-morning sun: armoured figures with swords at their hips, their chest-plates glinting like gemstones. They traipsed over the sands, back-dropped by a camp that streamed smoke into the pale blue sky. Across the frontage of the tents, the tiny dots of soldiers and servants could be seen circling frantically, attending to tasks and issuing orders to prepare for what came next. From afar, it was little more than a blur – but across the faces of the soldiers who approached, the army's whim was writ large in their harsh glares.

They are here to win, My'ala assessed. *They are here to conquer... no matter the victims left in their path.*

Stood on the dune-crest on the western side of their village – with the glistening oasis at her back, bordered by the palm trees and swaying reedbeds – My'ala rolled her shoulders and pressed her tongue to the roof of her mouth. The sun beat down overhead, forming sweat across her brow. The drum of her heart thundered in her ears, nearly bursting from her chest. At her sides her hands clenched and unfurled, awaiting the arrival of the soldiers. Awaiting the arrival of her fate.

There's no going back.

For a moment, she glanced behind her and took in the scene, swallowing over a lump in her throat as she did so. Flanking her on either side, the God-Elect's personal guards stood to attention, watching the approaching soldiers with a look of disgust and ire. Beyond them, she saw some of the villagers waiting further down the ridge: the few brave – *or foolish* – souls who had left the comfort of their homes to witness the events unfold. They watched her expectantly; quiet prayers escaped their shaking lips. And beyond them...

Our home, My'ala thought, the sand falling away beneath her as she struggled to stay standing. She saw the waters and the fishing huts; the storehouses and the prayer chambers; the guard posts and the armouries; the firepits and the torches. Their family home, up on the ridge to the south. The tiny birds, dancing along the alcoves of the roof there.

They had built it from nothing. Raised it from the very stones at their feet. They had carved the wood and chipped the rocks and sewn the nets to catch the fish. They had built the fires and sung the songs, and built the instruments to give them life. Elders had passed and been buried there; children had been born and raised there, calling it their only home. Her own daughter, Ki'lu, was a born nomad. A citizen of New Arbash. The waters of the oasis, and the sands of the dunes, were the only places she had ever known. They had built it from nothing, and in five years it had become like home. Not Arbash, but something very close to it.

A place we can live... and be free.

Turning back to the west again, her heart became stony. Her eyes narrowed, her sword burning against her hip. Her gaze fell on the central figure amongst the approaching soldiers: a ginger haired man in a deep blue robe, with silver rings glinting on his spindly fingers.

She had been told stories when she was younger about the evil in the world: stories she had then told Ki'lu, to keep her safe and wise of danger. Those stories had originated from Arbash, many of them from the paintings that scaled the God-Elect's palace. The monsters that featured there had been carved on the figureheads of the city fountains; the narratives, too, were written in the literature of the long-lost, back when the Prophets had still walked the deserts and Arbash had only just formed. Every elder remembered the stories, and every child feared them: the tales of great beasts and enormous scorpions and cruel people with swords and green eyes. They were warnings to protect the weak. To many, they were nothing but myths.

But, watching the Headman cross the sand dune just ahead of her, their face straightening into a fickle grin, My'ala saw it differently. She saw the truth beyond the narrative. The origin of the stories. Evil was not something left to the imagination.

It walks and it breaths, like all the rest of us.

My'ala took a step forward and pulled her cowl down, letting her hair billow in the westerly wind. She pressed her hand against her waist, revealing the sword beneath her robes. Her face, aglow with sunlight, possessed a radiance that rivalled the sunrise. Rivalled the stars themselves. She thought of

Nehebu for a moment, and swallowed the pain down with a hiss.

This is my fight, she proclaimed.

Now, I must win it.

On the opposing ridge, the Headman lifted a hand and his soldiers drew to a halt. They rested their hands on their sword hilts, sneering at her with disgust. Taking a step forward, Nero met her gaze and smiled.

"Hello *My'ala*," he said.

"Nero," My'ala grimaced, her voice level and firm.

"You know, I was half expecting that you wouldn't be here now… that you would have tried your luck out in the wastes, rather than face my army. A shame, really. I would have liked the *hunt*."

My'ala scoffed. "I suppose I should be sorry that I've disappointed you, Headman… but we are a people who defy the odds, so perhaps your ignorance is the real disappointment."

At her words, Nero's façade cracked momentarily. He clenched a hand and curled his nose up at her, before shaking his head. "It is rather unwise to try and make a fool of me, considering the *circumstances*," he growled. "You'd do well to remember that."

"You can do nothing."

"I can do a great many things, to the detriment of you and your people."

"Your threats don't scare me," My'ala challenged.

The Headman smirked. "Now look who's being the *fool*…"

"I'm not here for games, Nero." She gestured to the sandbank behind her, and the village that lay beyond. "I know what you're here for."

"As if it was for any other reason... I would not waste my time in such a place if there wasn't something to *covet* first."

"This land is not for you. It never has been."

"Ah, my desert gem, but it *will be*." He waved a finger at her. "It will be, and you... you had your chance to escape that fate! To be free of what comes next! You could have fled into the deserts; you could have tried your luck reaching the huge river to the south. You had your chance... and you squandered it. You failed."

"I have failed *nothing*," My'ala growled. "This is our village. This is my home. You forced us out of our last one, when you arrived at our shores with your boats and your swords. But this will not be the same. It cannot be so. I would sooner fall to every sword you have, than abandon what we've built here."

"That can be *arranged*." Nero flashed his teeth.

Unperturbed, My'ala maintained her stance, staring down the hunched figure in his dark blue robes. She did not move, and did not react.

The Headman scowled. "I don't want to harm any of you, you know that."

"Weak words... for a man who comes with swords."

"But why all of *this*?" His frustration flashed to the surface, as he jabbed a hand out in her direction. "Why this defiance? What could possibly mean so much to you here, to warrant risking your life for it?"

My'ala ground her teeth. "Because this is our *home*."

"And what? It's just a bunch of houses, and a lake... what makes it so special?"

"Because we sacrificed *everything* for this," she exclaimed, her voice rising like the crests of the dunes. "We gave our lives, and our livelihoods, for this place. We built the homes and grew the crops and farmed the fish. We weathered storms and droughts and every force of nature. We came together as a people – as survivors in this bleak land – and we overcame. We survived, and we prevailed, in spite of everything..."

"To eke out a living in this dusty hovel, in the middle of nowhere?" Nero sneered, licking his lips. "Such a tragedy..."

"We had no *choice* because of you."

"You had every choice... and now you find that freedom, even with a price paid, is not *guaranteed*."

Nero took a step forward; My'ala flinched, almost prizing her sword from its scabbard. Over the ridge behind her, she heard the God-Elect's guards shift in their armour.

"You could have been so much more, My'ala," the Headman mused. "You could have been one of my leaders. A governor, or a landlord. You could have ruled your people for me. Under my wing, you could have had whatever you wanted..."

"I would never sacrifice my people to the likes of *you*," My'ala spat. "They deserve so much more than that fate."

At that, Nero produced a grin that made My'ala shiver with unease. "Oh, don't worry... you and your people are destined for *far* more than just being my subjects."

My'ala frowned. "What do you mean?"

"You see, I have a building project I need to complete... a harbour, in that pretty little cove you people love so much... and I need workers to do it. And lots of them. Workers who are fine with long hours, little food and even less pay..."

"You would make us slaves?"

"The exact definition is often muddied." The Headman met her gaze. "But, call it what you will, you'll all be coming with me regardless... of your own volition, or in chains. I don't mind either way."

Behind him, the soldiers laughed in unison: puppets, pulled by the strings of their master. Nero seemed to draw strength from their amusement, lifting to his full height.

"We are going nowhere," My'ala proclaimed. "This is our home, and here we shall remain."

The Headman lifted an eyebrow. "And if you are not given a choice?" he asked.

"Then we shall fight."

"Ah, but who is this '*we*' you really speak of, My'ala?" Nero opened his hands out, challenging her, an arrogance coating his skin like algae. "Who is *we*, in this scenario? Your people? The citizens of this squalor? Who are they to you, My'ala? Who are *you*, in all of this? Do not forget the terms I gave you, when I first came here: that I would return in three days, with my soldiers in tow—"

"Awaiting my answer to the question: '*what are we?*'" My'ala smirked, watching Nero baulk at the interruption. "I remember your terms, Headman... I remember what was promised. An answer, for our freedom."

"A *good* answer, for the *chance* of freedom." He clicked his tongue. "Do not forget that, my little desert gem... I am not a man to be bluffed."

My'ala bit her tongue, swallowing her fear. "So be it."

Nero studied her for a moment with an insidious twist of his mouth. "Well in that case, My'ala, tell me..." Stooping low, he cocked his head at her like a vulture. "...what *are* you, and your people, and why do you deserve to be spared?"

My'ala tensed and felt her vision shift. Conversations from the previous day overlapped in her mind, a mosaic of tiles and colours. Nehebu's wisdom and her parents' love; Su'la's intuition and the God Elect's faith. The mosaic flowed in her head, behind her eyelids, drawing heavy on her breath. Like the rippling waters of their oasis.

A beauty of their own.

Ki'lu's face filled her thoughts. Her smile and her laugh and the knots of her hair. Splashing about in the oasis; asleep on Aurelius's shoulder.

For my little hummingbird.

My'ala opened her mouth.

"My father would say that we are born of the sand, and that to the sand we return when we depart this world," she began. "To someone like yourself, Headman, that may be a perfect answer: to lead a life so indiscriminate, where without doing anything more, you are free to do as you wish. I could perhaps end my answer there, and satisfy your wish. But my father didn't mean it that way... and I suppose, neither do I. He didn't look at life and who we are, solely through the lens of a life born and a death buried. He never has, even when he was so close to death himself. For him, our lives are defined by what connects those two points: the bridge that we all walk across, in search of who we are.

"And there's so much to find in that journey. There's so much to love. We are our souls, caught on the desert winds, striving towards something greater than embodies us and makes us whole. For some, that is found by our own will; for others, that is by the grace of the God. But people can't deny it... they can't deny the feeling of seeking out something more: something to fulfil them, to expand their minds and feed that urge inside. We are thinkers and doers, after all: our lives are in constant motion. Even stopping is a choice... because to stop and reflect, is to take time for what comes after.

"But we live in that motion. We embrace it; it *is* who we

are. We learn and grow. We adapt and prevail against adversity. We look after each other, and strive to an ideal greater than ourselves. How fast we go, or how far we climb… it's all in our own journey. We need not fear the path we are on…"

Because it's the path we choose… we are in control.

"We are guided towards love," My'ala continued. "We are guided towards hope, and community. We are dutiful, and selfless. We aspire to do good by our neighbours; by our elders and our friends. Family and faith connect us. What we give, is so much more important that what any of us can ever take. Those are the foundations that make us who we are. Those are the beliefs we all hold deep inside, no matter who we are, or how lost we become. They define all of us; they embody all of us. And the only choice we face, is the *how*: how to live, and define what our futures hold.

"Because we face threats at every turn." My'ala saw Nero's expression and smiled. "We face challenges that can make us lose sight of who we are. We can make choices that harm rather than aid the people we are and the communities we live amongst. We lose our respect and our duty; we become self-obsessed, and sometimes negligent. We become servants not only to others, but also to our worst intentions.

"But these things don't define us. They are reminders, to reconsider our actions. Every choice we are faced with, is a chance to do things differently than before. To honour who we *really* are, at our core as individuals. Because although we may come from the sand, and return to the sand when we pass… that soul we held, will live on in memory and affect the very ground we walk upon. Our fates, all of us, are intertwined, and affect one another every day."

My'ala pressed a hand to her heart, and gritted her teeth. "So let us choose love, hope and family. Let us choose grace, kindness and faith. Let us be the force of change we are always destined to be. Thinkers and doers; learners, and adapters. Let us find the greater purpose that we all aspire to achieve. Let us live on."

She breathed deeply.

"Let us... be *free*."

Around them, the winds fell away. The sand stopped rolling beneath their feet. Overhead, the blue and the white of the sky seemed to swell with beautiful tones.

My'ala stood, defiant, upon the western sandbank of the village. She held her gaze, held her stature as if hewn from marbled stone.

Before her, the soldiers who had arrived looked amongst each other in shock. They appeared suddenly smaller, their hands falling away from their sword hilts. At the crest of the ridge, the pride they had arrived with seemed to spill out over the sands.

And beneath them, their leader glared at My'ala, his face consumed with rage.

"I give you the chance at freedom... by answering just one *simple* little question... and you take that opportunity to *defy* me in this way?" he bellowed, incredulous. His hands shook violently, a red pallor filling his cheeks. "You dare challenge my authority, at the cusp of your end? You dare mock me, in front of my own *people*!"

"You were never going to let us walk free from this," My'ala retorted. "You were always going to invade: to *covet* us, as you call it. Your greed would have allowed nothing else. So why should I not speak my truth? Why should I not defy you, and *everything* you stand for..."

His robes flushed as he jabbed a hand out. "You have no idea what you've done."

My'ala shook her head. "I know exactly what I've done, Headman. I've stayed true to *who I am*... and that's what you wanted, wasn't it? To know who I am? To know who *we* are?" She cocked her head at him, belittling him. "Although I wonder, with the life you've lived... could you do the same? With the soul you've built, and the enemies you've made... could you really tell me *exactly* who you are?"

He flashed his teeth like a dog. "I have power... I have subjects, and peoples across the desert... I have cities and wealth *beyond* imagination..."

"And yet, inside... what do you have left? What is there left of you—"

"You cannot speak like this to me!"

"Why?" My'ala shrugged. "For fear of what? Of your tyranny? It is *hollow*, Headman. Hollow, and without the strength to *bite back*."

Nero seethed, his face creased with rage. He swung round to face his soldiers. "What are you waiting for? *Seize her!*"

They looked between one another, clenching and unclenching their hands. So afraid, suddenly, of where they were – of *who* they were. Not one of them reached for their blade; not one of them took a step forward.

"Fine!" the Headman barked. Reaching forward, he snatched one of their swords from their scabbard. "I'll just have to do it *myself*..."

Turning back to My'ala, Nero took three wading steps down the dune-side towards her, sweat sheening his face and dripping down his neck.

"*You're mine now, My'ala!*"

Watching him, My'ala bristled but held her ground. Her sword seemed to pulse at her hip. Behind her, she heard the God-Elect's guards unsheathe their blades.

The Headman continued to advance. The air grew thinner. The guards behind him began reaching for their own weapons again—

When the entire desert seemed to shudder beneath them, and Nero drew to a halt.

"What was *that*!" he shouted, twisting suddenly with his sword clasped tight in his hand. Beneath them, the vibrations became louder and more intense, until the dune-sides began to shift in waves. Nero stood swaying, the red fury in his face shifting to the sickly white of fear.

Hearing the sounds, My'ala stifled a gasp. Her heart lifted, reaching for hope.

"*What's happening!*" the Headman wailed, facing north—

Where the desert suddenly parted.

And the Sand-King emerged.

From beneath the ridge, the Dragon Prophet appeared, robed in plumes of dust. Lifting from the depths, their scales glistened: vast bronze shields scintillating in the sun. Amber eyes scoured the landscape. From between their curved teeth, the embers roared.

Channelling towards the Headman, Nehebu's jaws prized open like ancient doors. Within, flames licked, and guttural bellows issued from their throat. In one moment, Nero was stood between the dune-crests, staring up at the beast that consumed his vision.

And in the next, with a bellow of fear, he fell into the Sand-King's jaws.

My'ala stood in shock. Her eyes, propped open, struggled to process what she had seen.

Nero was gone. The Headman, who had harried their village for three days, was no more. The cruelty and despair that he had exacted on thousands, disappeared with a flash of fire.

Nero was gone.

It's over, she rasped, barely comprehending.

And the Sand-King has returned.

On the opposing ridge, the soldiers stared up as Nehebu rounded on them. They cowered beneath their formidable size, and whimpered as the Sand-King snarled and snapped. For a moment, they were frozen in place, grappling to one another with some false hope of solace.

Until Nehebu opened his maw again, and the flames licked about his pearlescent teeth – and the remaining soldiers, once full of such pride, turned tail and ran back towards their distant camp.

With their departure, an eerie silence returned to the dunes around New Arbash. A sense of conclusion, where sound became absent. There had been no violence; there had not even been a clash of swords. There was only the whisper of the wind, the crackle of Nehebu's embers.

And the steady rhythm of My'ala's heartbeat, tapping in her ears.

"You came," she said, looking up to the Sand-King. "Even though you said you wouldn't... why?"

Twisting their neck, Nehebu peered down at her, their scaly jaws lifting into a smile. *"Because your bravery inspired me, little mouse,"* they said. *"To stand against the Headman as you did... to say what you said, knowing it would only invoke his wrath... shows a strength of character greater than I have known of your kind. You stayed true to yourself – to* who you are, *as we have spoken of – and, with that… who was I to turn away in cowardice? Who was I to deny you the help you deserve?"*

My'ala bowed her head to the Prophet, fresh air filling her chest. "Thank you, Nehebu."

"*Always, My'ala.*" They paused, rolling their tongue over their lips. "*Besides, I was rather hungry… and ridding cruelty of this world fills one up most pleasingly.*"

My'ala laughed, and pressed her hand to her chest, over the warmth that she had come to associate with her soul. The kindred spirit within her; the source of all things that guided her forward. In that moment, she sensed its warmth as that of contentment and ease.

We have prevailed, she thought, nodding her head. *We have overcome, together.*

Turning, she pulled her robes together and ascended the small incline to the crest of the dune. Once there, she looked out on the people beneath her: the guards and the elders and the children gathered to watch. The people who had relied on her; those who had sacrificed everything to make New Arbash their home. They looked up at her, at the crest of the dune, with bewilderment in that moment. They looked past her, to Nehebu's towering form beyond, and shied away with fear alight in their eyes.

But there is nothing to fear. My'ala pursed her lips. *We are safe here at last.*

Her people saw her, stood with the Sand-King at her back and a sword at her hip. They saw her as a brave figure: a hero from all of the stories told to children before bed. A beacon of their hope; a guiding light across the dunes.

Because that was the truth beyond the narrative. The origin

behind the stories. That heroes, no matter who they were, were not something left to the imagination.

They walk and breathe, like all the rest of us.

Stood before her people, and the place they called home, My'ala lifted her fist to the air and roared with joy.

All around her, across the basin of the village, the citizens of New Arbash rallied to her cries, lifting their fists and hailing their victory beneath the beautiful glow of the sun. Guards and workers; elders and the young. All lifting their hands in unison.

Hope and community. Love and faith. My'ala closed her eyes. *To live on. To live free.*

The bridge, to what the future holds.

XIV

DISTANT SANDS

Three days later…

Stood on a dune-crest looking west towards the horizon, with Ki'lu holding her hand tightly next to her, My'ala watched the last of the soldiers' caravan gather their supplies and prepare to depart, a number of their camel-drawn carts already disappearing over the furthest ridges of the Unknown. Their tents had been disassembled, and their canopies packed into sacks and crates. The smoke stacks that had once sprouted from their ovens had grown cold and still. Shorn of their armour, the soldiers moved about the old camp miserly. It was like a great stain: where once there had been a black smudge, the desert sands had wiped it clean.

Much had happened, since the soldiers and the Headman had trekked out towards their village. It had all moved so quickly, that My'ala found she had barely had the time to catch up. Shortly after the confrontation with Nero – and the grand entrance of the Sand-King, from which the Headman had met his sudden, fiery end – a single soldier had returned from the camp in the distance, atop a lone camel. They had moved towards the village at great speed, the camel's pads kicking up dust and sand. At first, the guards of New Arbash had rallied; Nehebu, circling nearby, prepared their formidable return. But, rather than heralding bad news, the soldier had simply deposited a letter on the outskirts of their village, before turning tail and fleeing back to the camp as fast as their camel could carry them.

Collected by one of the guards, the letter had been taken to My'ala and the God-Elect immediately, who had opened it with a degree of caution to read the contents inside. Within, My'ala found a short proclamation, which she had read with eyebrows raised in astonishment: the soldiers would not only leave the area, returning to the distant walls of Arbash, but promised out of fear that they would never return again, allowing My'ala's people to be free. In a single missive, all of Nero's masterwork had been wiped clean. The soldiers, who had followed behind the Headman like dogs, had chosen with their newfound autonomy to forgo their master's wishes. The threat to New Arbash – to everything they had built – was snuffed out like a candle. They were safe, and they were free.

The days of terror were at an end.

Upon reading the news, the gathered guards and villagers had pumped their fists and embraced one another. Word had spread fast, and from the guard-towers to the prayer-house, celebrations had risen from every street corner. From sand-stone cellars, bottles of wine had been brought out, having been carried all the way from Arbash. As dusk fell, the fires were lit, and instruments were brought back out of hidden compartments. That evening, New Arbash had come alive with song and merriment: beneath a crescent moon, with threads of jade sweeping ethereally through the dark. Their fears had been allayed; the people let their relief be known through their voices and their hearts. Long into the night, the festivities had reigned, scintillating over the waters of the oasis – while in the distance, the soldiers had begun their deconstruction, preparing for the long journey back to the city by the sea.

And that was three days ago... much has changed since.

Looking out on them then, shifting huge canopy poles onto wood-framed carts, My'ala still maintained the small sense of disbelief she had felt when reading their letter. Part of her still thought it was all a ruse: that from somewhere, the army would return and seek their vengeance. That retribution would be meted on them for the loss of their defiant leader. That would have been the Headman's wish, she knew: that in his passing, he would have demanded his soldiers fight on and win. To retaliate, and leave nothing behind, for the glory of a kingdom many of them hardly knew.

But they are not Nero, My'ala thought, shielding her eyes from the glare of the sun. *They simply followed him. They became part of him: leaves of a burning tree. They abandoned who they were – who they could have been – because of him.* She pursed her lips; a brush of wind pulled up her back. *He was their only answer. And now that the anchor has been lifted... they are without answers. They have no one to follow, no one to delegate their lives to. They are adrift on a vast blue sea. So naturally, when faced with such an unknown, they have chosen look inwards...*

...and whether by fear or instincts of the soul, they have chosen to

show mercy, and go. They have chosen to preserve themselves, where once they had only seen sacrifice. They have come together as one; decided, for the betterment of all.

My'ala let loose a long breath.

They have chosen light... even after so long in darkness.

"Where are they going?" Ki'lu asked from beside her, clutching at the hem of her dress. At the end of My'ala's arm, she seemed to long to walk off over the dunes to see the soldiers in the distance: to ask them every question under the sun, curious without fault. To understand; to *learn*, most of all. My'ala saw it in her eyes, in the steady sliding of her feet in the sand.

Just like I was, on the first day I left the city walls, she thought, smiling. *Going fearlessly off into the world, with nothing but wonder in my eyes.*

"They're going home, my little gojan fruit," My'ala explained. "Back to where they came from."

"But is that not their home?" she asked, pointing to the empty dip where their camp had once stood.

"No, Ki'lu, that isn't their home." My'ala crouched down next to her daughter. "They travelled here, and made a home for a little while out there, on the sand. Not their real home, but... a temporary one."

"But..." She puzzled for a moment. "But... what is *home*?"

Opposite her, My'ala's smile grew wider, her thoughts filled with water wells and jade robes and deep sunsets on distant sandbanks. "Home... is what the people make it," she replied, brushing a hand over Ki'lu's hair. "Home is not a place. It's an *idea*. The people, and how they live together... like a family."

"Our family... is it home?"

My'ala nodded. "Yes, little hummingbird." She leaned down and kissed her on the forehead. "Our family is home. Your da, and Su'la, and your great-parents… we're all home. The whole village is home."

"And those people… out on the sand… will they go to their home, with their family?"

My'ala looked out to the caravan of soldiers in the distance, contemplating. "I think they will, yes. I think they'll go home, and they'll be with family…"

But it won't be the home they remember… and they won't be the same people who left, she thought. *It will be different, beyond what they can expect. Because they left as puppets to a madman… but they'll return as individuals, trying to rediscover who they are.*

And in that, I wish them only the best.

"Will they come back?" Ki'lu asked, her curiosity suddenly mixed with fear. "They had swords, ma-ma…"

"They won't come back little one, I promise," My'ala reassured. "They're leaving now, and we'll stay here. We'll be safe, don't worry."

"Did they say so?"

"Yes, in the letter they gave me. You remember the letter?"

She nodded, scrunching her dress. "They're going away. Is it because of that… *monster*… that you know?" Her eyes scoured the dunes momentarily – no doubt imagining the Sand-King's huge body emerging from somewhere, covering the entire world. Although she knew deep down that there was nothing to fear from the Dragon Prophet, My'ala understood how the stories of Ki'lu's childhood prompted fear first and foremost.

Which is still good, My'ala considered, *as one day, she may encounter something not-so-pleasant, and that fear will save her life.*

"That is part of it, yes," she admitted, not wishing to feign ignorance to her daughter. "The soldiers have lost their leader... and they had a change of heart... and with the Sand-King around, they won't come close to us. Don't worry."

"So the... Sand... King... they help us?"

"Yes, for certain. They're one of the good ones. One of my... *friends*, shall we say."

"Are they all good ones?"

"I'm not sure, my little gojan fruit... but if I find any, I'll ask and let you know." My'ala gave her daughter a wink.

Ki'lu nodded again, glancing to the remains of the camp again. "And the monster... will they stay, and help us?" she asked. "Will they protect us...?"

My'ala opened her mouth, going to speak before the words actually registered in her mind – sealing her lips again, as a hollowness filled her heart and emptied her lungs. She sensed inevitability; she sensed sorrow. The past few days had shown her just how uncertain the future had become.

But some things will always happen. She closed her eyes.

And some journeys must come to an end...

Embracing a brave smile, My'ala stroked her daughter's hair again, curling the thick braids between her fingers. "Your da and the villagers are all gathering on the ridge to the north now," she said softly, pointing to the oasis behind them. "I think we should go and join them, don't you?"

Ki'lu hesitated for a moment – her sense of curiosity still waylaid by the soldiers in the distance – but after a while she nodded and turned around, her skirt flowing in the breeze. "What's happening there, ma?" she asked. "Why is everyone going there?"

"You'll see, little mouse, don't worry." My'ala swallowed over a lump in her throat; she turned towards the oasis, and the village beyond. "Now come on, let's go find your da and the others. I'm sure they're all missing you lots."

Hand in hand, My'ala guided her daughter down the slope into the basin of their village, off towards the north ridge behind the reed-beds and the prayer-house. To go and greet their family; their fellow villagers and friends.

And to say goodbye to someone... for one last time.

XV

THE FUTURE

The entire village had gathered on the sun-kissed plateau overlooking the northern dunes, taking shelter under cloth canopies that billowed gently in the breeze. They spread out broadly in a crescent shape, their pastel-coloured robes like tiny pebbles on the sand. Children lay in their mother's arms, or wrapped about the legs of their fathers. Elders, congregating like ants, whispered amongst themselves with a wisdom forged over decades. Guards from the towers, still strapped in their armour, stood side-by-side with worshippers from the prayer-house. And at the centre of them all, the God-Elect stood stoically in his red-and-beige robes, looking out to the Unknown beyond like a captain aboard his longboat. He took a measure of the air in his lungs; closing his eyes, he let the sun's heat wash over his face.

"Are you ready for this?" he asked, exhaling in a long spout.

"I never know until it happens," My'ala replied, standing tall next to him. As she had approached the crowds, they had fallen away on either side of her like parting the sea, bowing their heads in acknowledgement to her and her daughter. My'ala had let Ki'lu lead as they crossed the plateau towards Aurelius: in the spotlight, she had looked up at the faces in amazement, shying away whenever anyone flashed her a smile. She found it bewildering, My'ala knew. Everything she had understood about the world had been flipped on its head. And so, as if tethering to what she knew, Ki'lu had refused to drop her mother's hand as they had meandered through the crowds – or at least, not until she had seen her father, and sprinted off to jump into his arms.

"Did you see the camp out to the west?" Aurelius asked, adjusting Ki'lu against his chest. "Looks like they're nearly all gone already."

"They were loading the last of the carts as we left," My'ala replied. "I imagine by dusk they'll be beyond the horizon… never to be seen again."

"And do you believe that that will be the end of them? That we'll actually never see them again?"

Slowly, My'ala nodded. "I do, yes, I… I think there's a lot of truth in it."

"How come?"

"The loss of their Headman has had a massive effect on them: they've lost a figurehead, and with it a sense of direction. This whole event will be put down to a madman's fallacy, I think: a journey that won't be told, but whose warnings will be found in bedtime stories."

"Not to repeat the same mistakes." Aurelius looked to the horizon.

"Exactly so," My'ala said quietly. "This has been a scary experience, and not one I ever wish to repeat again." For a moment, she glanced down at her daughter's beautiful eyes, and sensed the same uneasy knot of fear coil in her stomach. Her daughter had unknowingly survived a risk to her life, when Nero and his soldiers had approached New Arbash. She had been completely unaware of just how much danger she had been in at the time. Childish ignorance had saved her of that trauma: to her, the entire event would be nothing more than a strange dream.

But in the future, when she's older, My'ala thought, *she won't have that luxury. She'll be old enough to know... to understand, and remember. I don't want to repeat what has happened here for everyone's safety and freedom... but also to keep Ki'lu innocent of that worry for as long as I can.*

"We were lucky to have your wisdom," Aurelius commented, pulling her out of her thought. He reached over to squeeze her arm. "You did so well, facing up against Nero... challenging him when you knew the odds."

"I knew he would have tried to capture our village no matter what I said," My'ala admitted. "To a man like him, with morals so fragile and no sense of purpose beyond himself... there would have been no point trying to reason with him. So, I told him the truth."

"And it proved a truth so wise, that not even a Sand-King could refuse to get involved..."

My'ala snorted, thinking back to the moment Nehebu had breached from the dunes, swallowing the Headman and ending his reign of terror over the sands. "That may be true, yes." She rolled her tongue over her teeth. "Although there are not enough words in our language to thank them for what they did out there. When Nero came at us with his sword, I…"

Her mind ran for a heartbeat; Aurelius caught her, rubbing his thumb over her forearm. "He's gone now, though. We can consign him to a memory, where he belongs. That's what matters most."

My'ala reached across her chest and clasped his hand. "You're right… we're safe now."

"We are, and we will be from here on out." Aurelius turned to the north, and cocked his head out over the dunes. "Now, all that remains is the difficult part…"

My'ala followed his gaze, and swallowed.

The last goodbye.

Slowly – rolling over the dunes like a vast serpent – the Sand-King emerged from a plume of dust in the distance, their bronze coat shimmering in the spectacular light. Waves of sand split across their sides as they approached the village; at her back, My'ala heard gasps of awe from those gathered. The shock, to witness such a being: such a creature of myth, made flesh in the depths of the Unknown. As vast as New Arbash, towering higher than the tallest cliffs. The Dragon Prophet; their saviour.

Nehebu.

At the edge of the plateau, where the sandstone fell away to rolling dune-crests, the Sand-King drew to a halt and lifted their head from the ground, sensing the air with a forked tongue that laced through pointed teeth. Their amber eyes shone with formidable flame; a trickle of smoke rose gently from their nostrils, sliding over the bony ridges of their snout. Hanging high above the crowd of villagers, those gathered stood silent and star-struck.

Behold the Sand-King, My'ala breathed. *Behold the last great beast of the Unknown.*

Stepping closer to Aurelius, she embraced him and Ki'lu with heavy arms, planting a kiss on her daughter's curly hair. She smelled of pillows and sweet-cakes; the scent almost made My'ala cry.

Turning, she took a few steps forward towards the edge of the plateau, her robes sweeping beneath her like the petals of a cactus flower.

Her breath trembled in her throat. She felt the hot sun against her back. Above, the Sand-King lowed their massive head until their eyes were level with hers, reaching into the corners of her very soul.

"Nehebu," she said softly.

"*Little mouse,*" they replied, their voice mellow and deep like waves in a sea cave.

My'ala clamped her jaw. "I guess this is goodbye... isn't it?"

"*Like the sands brushing away footsteps so freshly placed, our journey together comes to an end. We are stars, orbiting one another... clinging to those moments of closest passing.*"

"Will we see you again, one day?"

"*To some questions I have no answers, My'ala... and that is one of them. I am ancient, and my embers are slowly growing cold. My life in this beautiful land is coming to an end. My nights are long, and my sleeps are deeper. I cannot know how long I have left.*" They paused, studying her. "*But if I know one thing, little mouse, it is that, if I do never encounter you again... I shall consider it an honour and a blessing to have had this time together. You are a spirit and a soul of such strength, and I pray the tremors of your heartbeat may grace this land for many long years to come.*"

"Thank you." My'ala swallowed again painfully. "But... I don't know what to do now, Nehebu. I don't know what the path is from here. When Artemis returned to the sand, on the day we left Arbash... and when Othella rose to the stars, when we arrived here five years ago... it felt like it wasn't the end. That there was still *more*, somewhere ahead of me. More to learn, to understand. More questions to answer in my soul. It was relieving, but now, here, with... with you, I..."

"*You realise the end is here,*" Nehebu finished, blinking slowly. "*That there is nothing more from hereon, but the life you now lead: the family you cherish, and the people you support. The village that you call your home, and the lessons you have learned along the way. Of the Prophets who joined you on this journey... from the first moments you set out from Arbash as a little girl... there will be no more. Artemis was the first... and I, little mouse, shall most likely be the last.*"

"But what if I need you?" Emotion tugged at her voice. "What if I have questions or... or if something happens to us? What if the soldiers return one day, with someone just as bad as Nero at the helm? I'll have no-one, I... I won't have someone to go to... to answer anything..."

"*That is not true, My'ala. Of course you will. You always will.*"

"But... who?"

The Sand-King – towering tall, wreathed in bronze – blinked slowly, thoughtfully. "*You have overcome so much in this life already, little mouse,*" they said. "*The Prophets who have joined you... they have guided you on this journey. They have held you close, and kept you safe... but someday, we have to let go. We have to let you find your own wings, like a bird taking flight... or like a little girl, stepping clear of her city walls for the first time.*" They looked out to the plateau behind her, to the people gathered there. "*These people, they look up to you. They believe in you. You have saved them, and given them hope in such dark times. You led them into the desert, and built a home for them out of nothing. You are their star, little mouse... you are their guiding light. We Prophets have taught you about life; about the family you keep, and the person you are... but now you, My'ala, must take up that mantle for yourself. You must be what you were always destined to be, since you first found the Hermit sat beneath the tree..."*

My'ala turned, and looked out on her people. Warmth filled her soul.

"A Prophet of the Unknown, My'ala," Nehebu exclaimed. *"The wisest of us all..."*

Amongst her people, My'ala saw wide eyes and looks of wonder. Expectation, and fortitude; hope, and peace. The bindings of community: family and forefathers. Loved ones and elders. Workers and mothers and guards and worshippers. Kindness and togetherness. Belief and faith.

They looked to her, and saw a leader. Someone to trust; someone to honour. The children saw her in their stories, fighting the evil in every shadowy corner.

Aurelius was ahead of her, his pride like an aura, filling his body and the blood in his veins. He had stood with her, and held her. He had championed her and every triumph in her life. He had built a life for her, with every bone in his body.

And she saw her daughter there, too, in his arms: watching My'ala as if she had stepped from the clouds, flanked by stars. As if the very sands had parted beneath her, opening a path for her to walk along. My'ala's breath filled her lungs, and tears prickled at the corners of her eyes: seeing herself as she had always hoped she would, in the curious rounds of her daughter's eyes.

Someone to be proud of... a mother to care. She placed a hand on her heart; Nehebu's words echoed back to her.

And now, a Prophet of the Unknown too.

"But what if I'm not ready?" My'ala asked the Sand-King. "What if it is too much, or... if I make a mistake?"

"*No-one is ever ready, little mouse,*" Nehebu replied. "*No-one ever knows every answer to what comes next. But they do not need to: the knowing does not make one a Prophet. It's the* trying *that defines us... it's the trying that allows us to succeed. This mantle is passed to you, My'ala, not because you have every answer... but because you have every question, and will do whatever you can to serve the needs of your people. Always unsure, but always determined. Faithful no matter what...*"

"But I'm so *scared*, Nehebu." My'ala wiped a tear from her cheek. "I'm so scared of the future. There's so much I don't know..."

"*You need not fear, little mouse.*" The Sand-King bowed their head to her. "*If there is one thing I have learned from our time together, it is that you can always defy the odds, and with love and kindness, you will always prevail. You have a strength within you that makes the very sands fall away at your feet. Never lose that, My'ala... never lose that strength in your soul. Hope is born in the tiniest places, but it grows from the biggest hearts.*"

My'ala nodded, and peered up into the fire of the Sand-King's eye. "I'll never forget you, Nehebu... you, or Artemis, or Othella. I'll never forget you, or what you've done for me. For all of us. I promise you that, on my life..."

"*I know, little mouse. You need not worry about that.*" Slowly, they lifted their head skyward. "*Besides, the good thing about us Prophets is that we are never truly gone... and if you ever find yourself wondering about what comes next, just look to the stars.*"

"I will, I... I promise." My'ala inhaled a shaky breath. "Thank you, Nehebu, for everything. Thank you for being here... for saving us."

"No, My'ala," the Sand-King replied, *"thank you for saving me. Thank you for showing me that, in spite of the Headman and those like him… your kind has the capacity for such love and strength. You have opened my eyes, and… when my time comes, I know I will return to the sands at peace."*

My'ala smiled, tears rolling down her cheeks. "It's been a pleasure, Nehebu. Thank you, always."

The Dragon Prophet bowed their massive head. *"Live free, little mouse. Never forget who you are… and never forget who you've become."*

With a rumbling deep within their throat, the Sand-King arced their head skyward and let fly an almighty roar, shaking the dust on the plateau beneath My'ala's feet. Sparks and embers flickered in the depths of their mouth, rising to lick around the points of their teeth. The last great beast of the Unknown bellowed.

Goodbye, Nehebu.

A heartbeat later, and they swung back down towards the dunes, gliding over the ridges in a massive plume of dust that coated the blue skies above. The bronze shimmer of their scales flashed in My'ala's eyes like seawater; their massive body snaked behind them, pulling apart the desert in their path.

My'ala watched them pass into the Unknown, slowly fading against the horizon. Like a figment of her memory; a tiny strand of her life slowly coming to an end. She breathed through it, her cheeks stained by tiny, translucent tears. Watching the Sand-King slip over a dune-crest.

Gone, forevermore.

Around her, she heard the quiet pad of footsteps approach. She felt the presence of others nearby, crossing slowly to the other side of the plateau. A few at first, then several – dozens, then several more.

Against her right leg, she felt a pair of tiny hands wrap around her thigh. Looking down, she saw Ki'lu's bushel of hair there, pressed against her robes. She held her tight; held her close, as if she would drift away on the wind. My'ala placed a hand against her head, stroking the ridge of her brow with her thumb.

At her sides, other hands wrapped around her shoulders and her arms. The familiar smell of her mother's incense filled the air, swelling in her heart like a flower blossom as her father clasped her free hand and whispered a prayer. On the opposite side, a head rested against her collar: out of the corner of her eye, My'ala saw the God-Elect's blonde hair tickle against her cheek.

Behind them, others appeared: villagers and their children. Faces with names, and ones she couldn't quite place. Young and old; broad and thin. Pastel robes like seashells over the pale white of the sands.

They gathered around her and locked their arms. Side by side, they stood and looked up to her. Their souls intertwined like a spider's-web, with the children rushing forward to join Ki'lu at her waist.

My'ala looked out on them, and found her breath catch in her throat. The tears warmed around her eyes. She sensed the emotions and thoughts flooding through them all: the hope; the family; love and faith; belief. In every draw of air and beat of their heart. Unequivocal, and absolute.

The core of who we are.

My'ala remembered Artemis. She remembered Othella, and Arbash. She remembered Nehebu the Sand-King, emerging from the sands by the rocky outcrop.

She remembered the white tree by the clementine groves. Losing Dur'al, and leaving her home. Watching her father contract illness, and nearly die before her very eyes.

She remembered the oasis where they settled. The New Arbash they now called home. The day Ki'lu had been born, and lay sleeping in her arms.

The journey she had been on. The lessons she had learned, and the dreams she had lived.

My'ala closed her eyes, and felt the sun warm her face.

This chapter ends, she mused.

And now, a new one begins...

EPILOGUE

THE PROPHET'S STAR

The reeds rose up around her like the points of sewing needles, rustling in the gentle breeze that lapped over the waters of the oasis. The panicles – browning in the heavy sun, full of feathery seed-heads – swayed against the blue of the midday sky. Thick leaves running up the stem created good cover against the sun, casting shadows over the soft earth underfoot.

Sat with her legs crossed, Ki'lu circled her finger through the soil in front of her, feeling the soft clay and dirt pull away from her fingertip. Occasionally she would find a small stone or pebble, which popped from the ground like a grain kernel and skittered off into the reeds. Other times, her finger would jump over the gnarled roots of one of the nearby plants: either the spindly undergrowth of the reedbed itself, or one of the larger roots from the palm trees on her left.

Ki'lu was not alone, either, in the small valley between the giant rushes: dragonflies as big as her hand circled overhead, buzzing and hovering sporadically in search of their next meal. They were wreathed in plates of blue and gold, with wings that looked like stained-glass windows in the light. Circling, they passed small flies and thick-shelled beetles on their path. Landing on giant leaves, they encountered desert-faring crickets, who sat on the stems and chirped rhythmically to one another. Skimming close to the ground, they darted clear of orb-eyed toads secluded in the dark, their warty skin blending with the clay-brown thickness of the soil.

Lifting her finger, Ki'lu giggled as the dragonflies buzzed closer to it, studying her muddied nail inquisitively. A few came close to landing – extending their six tapping legs to gain a foothold – but darted clear soon afterwards, as a lumbering beetle hummed past and disturbed their exploration.

Funny bugs, Ki'lu thought, bringing her hand back down to her side.

Looking down to her lap, she traced her finger over the ground next to her again, and assessed the roll of reed-paper nestled between her legs. She had carried it with her when her mother and Su'la had left the house that morning, joining Su'la on her expedition to explore the reedbeds for animals. She had followed her mother for most of the morning – turning stones and rummaging through the roots of the reeds – but after a while, Ki'lu had grown bored and decided to go on an adventure of her own: one where she could sit and do some drawing.

And not look at stupid rocks.

Across the reed-paper's surface, several long, sweeping lines and thicker blotches had been marked on the paper, where

Ki'lu had used the clay-mud to draw little shapes and designs. At the paper's edge, her tiny fingerprints dotted the page, too, where she had forgotten to wipe her hands on the hem of her dress.

Applying her fingertip again, Ki'lu pressed against the grain of the thick paper, adding some final touches to the design with her tongue poking between her clenched teeth. She was completely focused on her work; enraptured by the process.

Not noticing, as the reeds parted just ahead of her, and a figure stepped into the clearing with her.

"Ki'lu... is that you?"

Startled, Ki'lu pulled the paper together and looked up suddenly, her heart in her throat. Against the glare of the sun, she blinked up into the shadow – and frowned.

In a large red robe, a man stood watching her, his face concealed by the brow of his cowl. He was tall and thin, not too dissimilar to the towering reeds at his back. All that could be seen of his complexion were the thick curls of a grey beard spilling from his chin – that, and a small pipe hanging from his mouth, which trailed a line of smoke around the panicles above.

Confused, Ki'lu rose to a stand, keeping a close eye on the man. She sensed a familiarity there, but one that she couldn't place.

"Who are you?" she asked, clutching the reed-paper tightly against her chest. "Why are you here?"

Although she couldn't see his face, she sensed the old man smile. "I... am a traveller, my dear," he said gently, his voice soft and echoing like her mother's. "And I am here, because your mother is very worried about someone... a little adventurer who went out exploring and didn't come back.

Would you know anything about that, Ki'lu?"

Sheepishly, Ki'lu turned her cheek, which grew faintly red. "Is she... mad at me?"

"No, she isn't mad my dear. She could never really be mad at you. She got mad at me once, you know, but we worked it out eventually." He nodded, looking back through the reeds where he had emerged. "I'm sure you'll be just fine."

"How do you know my mamma?"

"From a very long time ago, little flower... back when your mother was very young. She'll tell you the story one day, I'm sure." In the shadow of their face, Ki'lu saw a flicker of light like a thousand stars, disappearing as fast as it had appeared.

"Where is my mamma?"

"She's just through here, my dear." Reaching over, the old man parted the reeds with a robed hand, opening a narrow channel through the rushes. As they fell away, Ki'lu heard the lilting cry of her mother in the distance. "She's waiting for you."

Ki'lu took a few steps forward and peered down the path through the reeds. Then, she looked up to the red-robed man next to her, and frowned again. "Are you not coming too?" she asked.

"No, Ki'lu, I'll stay right here," the old man replied. "You go see your mother. I'll be okay here, I promise."

Puzzling, Ki'lu nodded regardless. "Thank you, mister."

"That's okay, little flower." Ki'lu sensed them smile, a rush of wind passing over the reedbed above. "Now go on, don't keep her waiting..."

With a final glance to him, Ki'lu stepped over the roots and dashed through the reed-bed like a tiny mouse, clutching the thick paper to her chest. She stumbled several times – nearly toppling over into the mass of broad leaves – but kept her footing nonetheless, reaching the end of the reeds in a matter of heartbeats.

Ahead of her, she watched her mother turn to face her and gasp with relief, rushing over to her to check that she was okay. She pulled at Ki'lu's hair, checking her hands for scrapes or bruises.

"Are you okay?" My'ala asked, brushing dirt from Ki'lu's cheek. "Where did you go to?"

"I went into the reeds," Ki'lu explained. "I wanted to do drawing, but… I had no clay. I found some."

Her mother lifted an eyebrow, her face slightly cross. "I can see that, young lady. Look at your dress!" She pulled at the hem of the fabric, using her thumb to try and rub the dirt off. "That's a lot of clay…"

"I didn't want to make the drawing bad." Ki'lu tucked her chin against her collar. "I'm sorry…"

Looking deep into her eyes, My'ala relinquished her frown and smiled. "It's okay, my little hummingbird, it's okay. Just… let me know where you're going next time, okay? Then we can give you some old cloth to wipe your fingers on… not your very nice dress!"

Ki'lu nodded, understanding. "My fingers are dirty."

"That's okay, we can get them washed." My'ala squeezed her hand. "But, more importantly, I'd *love* to see the amazing drawing you did while you were out there… can I see?"

Sensing her mother wasn't really angry, Ki'lu brightened up and handed the thick reed-paper over. Navigating the edges, My'ala opened it on her lap and studied the drawings.

"Oh wow," she said, turning it into the sun's light. There were three designs there: three clay markings, with tiny points and thick smudges. "What is it, Ki'lu?"

Ki'lu pointed to the first one. "This one is a moon... but not the big one, the other one."

"A crescent?"

"Yea, a... a *cress-ent,*" she murmured, struggling with the word. Moving on, she pointed to the second one. "And this one... it's a sun. A big one."

"I can see... and this last one?" Her mother smirked. "Is that a toad?"

"That's a star, silly!" Ki'lu explained, giggling. "A big pointy star!"

"Oh, of course! How silly of me." Reaching up, her mother ruffled her hair. "And what made you draw these, Ki'lu?"

"They're big and pretty and I like them." Ki'lu sniffed and nodded her head. Then, she crossed her arms, stood tall like a little statue. "Do *you* like them, mamma?"

"Of course I do, my little gojan fruit," My'ala replied, admiring the artwork. "I think they're lovely. So lovely, in fact... that I know a perfect space on your wall to hang it up. What do you think?"

Ki'lu grinned, her heart almost ready to explode. "Yes!" she said, stamping her feet with excitement. "I want a whole wall full of them!"

"That sounds amazing, Ki'lu."

My'ala stood and held her hand out; Ki'lu clasped it gently, before looking up and down the ridge above them. "Where's Su'la?"

"Su'la has gone on ahead of us to do some more work... so I reckon we should head back to the house now and hang this up straight away. Then you can show your great-parents too: I think they'll *really* like it."

Ki'lu grinned again, nodding with glee. "Yes! Let's go!"

Watching her mother smile, Ki'lu followed My'ala as they navigated around the reed bed, the shadow of the palm trees falling across the sands next to them. A faint breeze pulled over the ridge above them, ruffling Ki'lu's dress like the tall reeds by the oasis.

Where I saw that man...

"Mamma?"

"Yes, Ki'lu?" My'ala replied. "What is it?"

"When you were small," Ki'lu said slowly, "did you meet lots of people?"

"A fair few, yes. Why?"

"Was one of them a man... an old man, with red robes... and a pipe with smoke?"

As the words fell from her lips, her mother stopped. Her hand tensed. An expression crossed her face that Ki'lu had never seen before.

"Did you?" Ki'lu tugged on her arm. "Who was he?"

Turning her head, her mother looked back to the reed-bed where they had come from. A sheen of tears coated her eyes, like two orbs of perfect glass. Then a smile filled her face, fuller and more beautiful than Ki'lu had ever seen.

"Mamma?"

My'ala looked down to her; she rubbed her thumb over Ki'lu's knuckle. "I did... yes," she said softly, as if the words were echoing up from her very soul. "I did meet a man just like that, when I was very young... young, just like you are now, and just as curious too."

Turning back to the path ahead of them, Ki'lu followed her mother again, their village slowly emerging from behind the spires of reeds.

"And when we get back home… I think it's time I told you a story, my little hummingbird," My'ala continued, looking up into the glorious blue sky. "A story about a man called Artemis the Hermit. A story of what it means… to *hope*."

THE END.

ACKNOWLEDGEMENTS

This book, as with its predecessors, came exactly when I needed it to, answering questions that I was asking myself about things too big to tackle alone. The Crescent Moon was borne at a time when I was working out what I was meant to do with my life; The Jade Sun came when I felt lost, and never quite at home. And the Prophet's Star, maintaining the trend, has given me direction in ways I hadn't expected: as to who I am, and what my future should hold as a man and as a writer.

Because this book was a journey. My life, during its writing, has followed a path of pain, hope and faith. The entire series, from My'ala's first steps in the vineyards of Arbash to hanging her daughter's painting in their home, has been an experience that has drawn out the core of who I am as a writer. I have cried a lot, and I have laughed, and I have embraced every moment of it. I have loved telling this story and sharing it with the world. And although My'ala's journey has come to an end, I am content with it: because the lessons we have learned together throughout this series, will endure long after these last words are written.

So, to that end, I will always be thankful: and to you, the reader, I will always be grateful.

‡

There are some people that I want to thank in particular, as well, who have helped with the process and publication of this book, bringing it to life as you see it now:

To Liam Fraser, my fantastic illustrator, who has embodied the spirit of the Prophets with their paperback covers and been a true friend at every turn;

To my friends and colleagues, who always asked for updates and have allowed me to celebrate this journey properly at its end;

To the indie book community, for every repost and review that has helped propel me to this crazy position I find myself in;

And to my family, particularly my mum and dad, who have helped me so much these last few months to show me the way forward and remind me of who I am. God bless you both; I love you so much.

‡

So, without further ado, I wish you all the best in your reading journeys ahead. I hope My'ala's journey has gifted something to you as it has done for me – in more ways than one!

Thank you, and as always…

Happy Adventures!

HONOURS LIST

Giving a massive thanks to:

Jennifer Sutton
Ross MacBaisey
Henry Sinclair
Glenn Dove
Ganesh Subramanian Alwarappa
Jake Wilson
Joseph McLachlan
Sean Doty
Claudia May
Joanne & Nick Guy
Rebecca King
Chris Fisher
Charlotte Macbean
&
Anton Heyward

For their support and contributions to the production and publication of this book and my future projects.
You are remarkable people, and have made a young man's dream come true.

I hope to do you proud.

www.ingramcontent.com/pod-product-compliance
Lightning Source LLC
Chambersburg PA
CBHW050328010526
44119CB00050B/722